Classification:

A Tool For Managing Today's Offenders

Perry M. Johnson, President
James A. Gondles, Jr., Executive Director
Linda H. Munday, Acting Director of Communications and Publications
Elizabeth Watts, Publications Managing Editor
Marianna Nunan, Project Editor
Jennifer A. Nichols, Production Editor
Ann M. Tontodonato, Cover Design/Stacey Raley, Mechanicals

ISBN 0-929310-90-X

Printed in the United States of America by Kirby Lithographic Company, Arlington, Va.

This publication may be ordered from:
American Correctional Association
8025 Laurel Lakes Court
Laurel, MD 20707-5075
1-800-825-BOOK

Contents

Foreword

Classification: A Tool for Managing Today's Offenders follows in the footsteps of the American Correctional Association's best-selling *Classification as a Management Tool*, which is now out of print. *Classification* is the only resource of its kind available to corrections professionals who need information on developing, implementing, and maintaining an inmate classification system.

Classification is an important, but often overlooked and misunderstood, area of corrections. The authors of the chapters that follow are all experts in the area of inmate classification. Readers are sure to benefit from the expertise and insight of these professionals. The broad scope of the chapters touch on a spectrum of issues surrounding classification, from legal issues to classification for women to risk assessment. Besides general discussions of classification issues, case studies of classification for internal management and objective classification give the reader a practical view on how specific classification systems work in specific environments.

ACA would like to thank all the authors for giving freely of their time and expertise. Special thanks go to Dr. Lorraine T. Fowler, Dr. Robert Levinson, and Larry Solomon for their help in reviewing the contents of this valuable book.

James A. Gondles, Jr.
Executive Director

I. The Revolution in Correctional Classification

By Larry Solomon and Alethea Taylor Camp

Classification is not a new concept in corrections. It has existed for at least 200 years under different names, but has always reflected the philosophy (e.g., retribution, incapacitation, and rehabilitation) of a particular era or cycle. Early in the nineteenth century, prisons took classification to one of its extremes when reformers isolated every inmate to allow each ample opportunity for introspection. This religious-style practice was intended to rehabilitate individuals for successful reintegration into the community. This philosophy was prevalent until after the Civil War when prison administrators turned to inmate labor to rehabilitate and punish.

As the twentieth century approached, running a prison system had evolved into a multifaceted endeavor that included political, administrative, and economic issues, as well as issues pertaining to the needs of inmates. Because labor was the major activity of most inmates, accruing income from inmate labor was the major goal of prison officials. Inmates' labor was necessary for the survival of most correctional systems. Rehabilitation did not become an objective of penology until the 1930s.

From the 1930s through the 1960s, various criminological and psychological theories of the causes of crime and delinquency developed. A number of practices emerged and dominated the criminal justice and correctional systems, ranging from treatment of mental disorders to vocational training. The underlying concept was that offenders could be rehabilitated. Chain gangs and road crews began to disappear as rehabilitation programs became popular.

In some systems program participation carried incentives, usually

---

Larry Solomon is deputy director of the National Institute of Corrections in Washington, D.C. Alethea Taylor Camp is a correctional programs specialist for the Prisons Division of NIC.

parole or "good time." Using classification to assess inmate program needs came into its own during this period because not enough resources were available to allow all inmates to participate. Although many programs (e.g., education, vocational training) were voluntary, this change was paralleled by the movement toward reintegrating offenders through community-based correctional programs. Because these programs often placed inmates at work or study in the community, the role of classification from the perspective of supervision, custody, and programming took on added significance. Classification became the main tool for balancing an inmate's rights not to deteriorate in prison and to be placed in the least restrictive custody level with society's right to protection from criminal behavior.

In the late 1960s and early 1970s, a number of trends and forces converged to raise serious doubts about the "rehabilitation ideal" and existing related prison practices. This convergence led to a revolution in classification from which objective classification systems emerged. These trends and forces included the following:

1. Inmate-initiated litigation resulted in court rulings that subjective classification systems were based on unfounded assumptions regarding inmate behavior and criteria that were not uniformly applied.

2. Substantial evidence showed that subjective systems tend to routinely overclassify inmates and unnecessarily place them in higher levels of security and custody than required by the risk they actually pose.

3. Because of pressure from prison crowding and diminishing fiscal resources, many prison systems became interested in objective classification in hopes that inmates who represent lower risk could be classified to lower security levels and community placements rather than being housed in expensive and limited higher security facilities.

4. Early research and evaluation were beginning to demonstrate that objective classification systems and instruments were more efficient than clinical judgment or intuition.

Concurrent with these findings was the public's growing concern about the increase in crime, particularly violent crimes. The environment was ripe for the reemergence of retribution and incapacitation as correctional philosophies and for growing interest in the concept of offender screening (e.g., focusing on systems that could efficiently predict which offenders represent higher security and custody risks). The courts and correctional administrators came to view classification as the key vehicle for making sound decisions regarding a number of areas in correctional administration and operations—among them security, custody, supervision, programs for offenders, and facility planning.

Growing sophistication in the social sciences, criminal justice, and the use of statistics for social research and evaluation made this period particularly ripe for change. Work in the late 1960s and early 1970s on predicting risk and screening offenders through objective classification provided specific models of how objective classification could be used for more efficient decision making. Corrections was eager for change and fully embraced this and other advances.

Before the development of objective classification systems, classification decisions were based largely on the subjective judgment, experience, or intuition of correctional practitioners. Decision criteria and factors present in objective classification were either very informal or not specific. The almost total lack of documentation and accountability of subjective classification systems contributed to inappropriate assignments of inmates, inconsistent decisions about similarly situated offenders, inefficient use of facilities and overclassification, lack of data for future program and facility planning, and the failure to carefully assess inmates and assign them to correctional programs and services.

Subjective classification systems dominated through the mid-1970s. In the mid- to late 1970s, objective classification systems began to appear. This "new generation" of classification systems caught the interest of the federal courts and the corrections community. Objective correctional classification systems developed in the late 1970s and early 1980s included the following attributes:

1. Classification instruments that contained criteria and factors for making decisions about security and custody were used—some were validated, most were not.

2. The same components and scoring were employed for all offenders, but they did allow some ability to override the criteria and components with justification.

3. Offenders were assigned to levels of security and custody

based on their backgrounds, prior criminal history, previous number of incarcerations, etc.

4. Correctional staff were encouraged to make similar decisions on similar offenders, and attempts were made to limit overrides to no more than 15 to 20 percent of the cases.

5. Planning and accountability were more efficient because data could be analyzed for better facility and program planning, and decisions were documented for systematic monitoring.

Ground-breaking work on objective classification and screening systems started in the early 1970s and provided models that would facilitate the acceptance of objective classification in three critical correctional areas: probation, prisons, and parole. The Wisconsin Division of Corrections pioneered an offender risk screening and needs assessment system that its probation units were using quite effectively, spurring the interest of many probation agencies nationally. The U.S. Parole Commission developed guidelines for parole decisions that articulated the commission's policy on parole release and brought structure to this area of correctional decision making. The Federal Bureau of Prisons created a work group that led to the development of an objective prison security and custody decision system and instrument for initial placement and reclassification of inmates.

Definition and Purposes of Objective Classification Systems

The improvements of correctional resource management are a major objective of offender classification systems. Toward this end, and partly in response to the crisis of prison crowding in the last decade, a number of classification trends have developed, including: increased emphasis on risk assessment; development of objective approaches to classification; the integration of needs assessment; and the use of a systems approach to management. Within each trend, the goal of effectively allocating scarce resources is balanced by pressures to achieve equity and accountability (Clements 1988).

As early as the mid-1970s, the federal courts recognized the importance of objective classification as a correctional management tool. Intervention by federal courts motivated many prison systems to reexamine the relationship between classification and the management and operation of prison systems. *Palmigiano v. Garrahy* (443 F.Supp. 956, D.R.I., 1977) provides a comprehensive overview of the value of classification to correctional management: "Classification is essential to the operation of an orderly and safe prison system. It enables the institution to gauge the proper custody level of an inmate, to identify the inmate's educational, vocational, and psychological needs, and to separate non-violent inmates from the more predatory. Classification is also indispensable for any coherent future planning."

Classification may be defined as a system and process that divides inmates into groups for a variety of purposes and considerations, including the following:

- to assess and group offenders for the purpose of designating security and custody

- to diagnose offenders and determine programs and services, such as medical and mental health services, vocational programs, educational programs, and work programs, based on their need and the availability of services

- to designate offenders for the appropriate housing placement within a facility or institution

- to schedule reviews of security, custody, and program placement and to reassess needs and progress for possible reclassification

- to assess inmates for placement in community transition programs and for special needs

In objective classification systems, classification decisions are based on explicitly defined criteria rather than on subjective judgments. The objective criteria are organized into a classification instrument accompanied by operational procedures for systematically applying the instrument to inmates. The objectivity of a classification system is a matter of degree because its creation involves subjective judgments, and all of the systems currently in existence incorporate at least some subjective staff judgment (Alexander & Austin 1992). According to Buchanan, Whitlow, and Austin (1986), the following conditions should be present in an objective classification system:

- classification instruments that have been validated for prison populations
- the same components and scoring/classification approach for all offenders
- decisions based only on application of factors shown to be related to placements
- assignment of offenders to a security classification consistent with their background
- similar decisions among individual classification analysts on comparable offender cases that minimize overrides
- inmate involvement
- easy to understand for both staff and inmates
- systematic and efficient monitoring capabilities

At the technical level, classification may be viewed narrowly as the mechanics, instruments, or techniques used to assess inmates and to generate recommendations about them. At a resource level, classification affects the allocation of resources (e.g., facilities, beds, jobs, services, and programs). At a policy level, classification may be shaped by or itself shape policy regarding those characteristics of offenders that are worthy of note. The factors included in a classification system imply their importance to correctional objectives. From management's perspective, classification offers tools to organize resources to achieve correctional objectives. The degree to which classification succeeds depends on the degree to which correctional administrators view it as useful and then use it (Burke & Adams 1991).

Classification should be placed in the context of overall correctional management as a major part of the overall administration and operation of a correctional system and its facilities on several levels. For agencies or departments, classification policy, goals and objectives, and procedures must meet the philosophy, resources, and needs of the agency or department. For facilities or institutions, classification policies help to assess and determine security, custody, and program needs, as well as to determine the movement and assignment of inmates from initial commitment through transition to community programs. Recognized as a major driving force in correctional management, classification has a major effect on specific areas of correctional management, including population and fiscal management, improved decision making, prison management and operations, planning and monitoring, and public safety.

Management of Crowded Prisons

Prison populations have increased significantly over the past ten years, exceeding 855,000 in 1992 (BJS 1993). Between 1980 and 1990 the prison population increased 134 percent and has continued to increase, although at a slower rate. By the end of 1990, state prisons were estimated to be operating at 115 percent of their highest capacities and 127 percent of their lowest capacities (Greenfeld 1992). Despite beds being added to the nation's correctional systems, the current prison capacity is rated at over 614,000 beds, or about 24 percent over capacity (Greenfeld 1992). These data clearly establish prison crowding and population management as one of the most critical problems confronting correctional systems today and into the foreseeable future. Overpopulation is not a problem that exists in isolation. Its consequences spill over into all areas of correctional operations, arousing concern about such issues as institutional security, the health and safety of staff and inmates, and compliance with court-mandated standards for care and supervision.

Classification cannot reverse the trend in increased prison population, but it can help administrators use institutional resources efficiently. With proper objective classification, only those inmates presenting a substantial risk to others are placed in costly, high security institutions, while those demonstrating less risk and a reduced need for supervision can be placed in lower security facilities. Appropriate classification may assist in determining which inmates can be considered for transition programs or early release into the community under proper supervision (Buchanan & Whitlow 1987).

Classification can also generate data about current and projected populations that can be useful in facility and program planning. Many institutions can be adapted to meet the prison population's needs based on information derived from analysis of classification systems. Such information can also lead to greater use of intermediate sanctions for nonviolent offenders who pose a limited risk. Although classification does not offer an easy answer to reducing prison populations, it is an effective vehicle for addressing this chronic problem.

7

Fiscal Management and the Effective Use of Limited Resources

Prisons are very costly, and they must be considered limited resources, especially in a climate of fiscal deficits, diminishing public resources, and other competing domestic priorities like education, health, and housing. Many states have tried to reduce crowding in prisons by increased spending, with overall spending on corrections nearly doubling in the past decade. In fiscal year 1992, the nation spent over $19.1 billion on corrections construction and operations (Camp & Camp 1992). This represents a 20 percent increase over 1990. Spending for corrections has climbed an average of 13 percent annually since 1986 and is absorbing much of the growth in state revenue.

Given the current dilemmas facing federal and state correctional systems—increased prison costs, deficits, and overpopulation—classification may be seen as a way to use scarce correctional resources more efficiently. Overclassification and misclassification tend to place a disproportionate number of offenders in costly maximum security beds that should be retained for only the most violent and difficult-to-supervise inmates. To overclassify and oversupervise is to misuse limited and expensive resources. In an era when program resources are becoming more scarce, objective classification can be one of the most effective ways to allocate those resources to achieve the best balance for the use of facilities and services consistent with a safe and humane correctional environment. The increasing demand for security and services calls for effective and efficient decisions about classification that make the most of physical, financial, and human resources.

Quality Decision Making

Objective classification systems should have the dual goals of contributing to equitable and consistent decisions and placing offenders under the least restrictive supervision and custody demonstrated by their level of risk. Objective classification systems have been credited with more consistent classification decisions and decrease in the number of staff errors, misinterpretation of classification policy, and overclassification (Alexander & Austin 1992).

Subjective classification processes have been criticized for their lack of documentation and lack of clear, explicit criteria for decision making, leading to an unstructured, arbitrary, and capricious process. *Laaman v. Helgemoe* (437 F.Supp. 318, D.N.H., 1977) specifically commented that classification systems "cannot be arbitrary, irrational, or discriminatory." The *Ramos v. Lamm* (485 F.Supp. 122, D. Colo., 1979) decision established that "any system of classification, placement and assignment must be clearly understandable, consistently applied and conceptually complete. Methods of validation must be completed."

Another consideration regarding the quality of the decisions is the principle of least restrictive custody or supervision, which holds that offenders should be placed in the least restrictive custody level that is commensurate with their own safety and the safety of other inmates, staff, and the community. This principle also relates to the pervasive problem of overclassification. Eliminating overclassification and oversupervision should be one of the most significant goals of an objective classification system, and it contributes to the appropriate level of security and custody for individual offenders.

Prison Management and Operations

An objective classification system contributes to the orderly management and operation of correctional facilities and is instrumental in fulfilling the mission and objectives of a correctional system. "Its purpose is twofold: to match offenders to current resources and to identify needed resources" (Clements 1988). Assessment risk and designating security and custody are the elements of a classification system that receive the greatest exposure and are generally equated with classification (Burke & Adams 1991), but classification systems must also focus on inmate needs for services and programs.

Decisions on custody, institutional transfer, and eligibility for community programs can be made by systematically coordinating information from the institution or facility and the central office. A department's classification system should consist of written policies and procedures that structure discretion by using objectively derived behavioral factors logically related to the decision being made and by adhering to a method to override or alter the classification decision that provides written reasons to justify this action. Classification determines the appropriate level of security and custody for each offender, thus decreasing the likelihood of abuse, fear, violence, and litigation among staff and inmates. It also provides the most efficient way to identify vocational, educational, medical, and drug abuse treatment needs for inmates as well as for other needs.

When the population of a facility or institution is large, violent, predatory, disorderly, and/or dangerous, the institution will focus most of its resources on security and custody. Rehabilitation is still a concern, but the institution has to set priorities, and under these conditions, security and custody concerns must be emphasized. With a prison population that is less violent, dangerous, and predatory, an institution can focus more of its resources on rehabilitation concerns. Physical restraints and concerns about adequate procedures and supervision still exist, but the emphasis is different (Burke & Adams 1991).

Correctional Planning and Monitoring

Data collected from an objective classification system can be extremely useful for planning programs and facilities, budgeting, and ensuring the system's accountability (e.g., monitoring and evaluation). In 1989, $6.7 billion was spent on prison construction; more than $2.7 billion was spent in 1992 (Camp & Camp 1992) Only nine states had no construction or additions to existing facilities planned during 1992. The average cost per prison bed is approximately $56,435, ranging from $36,000 for a minimum security bed to $75,000 per maximum security bed (Camp & Camp 1992). Even more troubling are the costs of operating correctional facilities. The cost of construction versus operational costs of prisons is striking. Every dollar spent for construction takes $20 to $35 to operate a facility or institution.

In a time when financial resources are diminishing and the costs of prison construction and operations are escalating, it is imperative that classification data be used for facility planning and budgeting. Over the past decade objective classification systems have been found to be effective in significantly reducing overclassification and in helping correctional systems plan the appropriate mix of intermediate sanctions and correctional facilities needed to supervise and house a specific offender population.

Classification systems also evaluate offenders to determine their need for medical, mental health, substance abuse, and educational services and programs. The information obtained from these assessments can be invaluable in planning and designing appropriate programs. The data could be used for program budgeting and for seeking other sources of funding. The number of special needs offenders—sex offenders, older offenders, and long-term offenders—also appear to be on the rise. The information produced through classification can help correctional systems better understand how changing populations may affect a system and plan accordingly.

Correctional system accountability is a growing issue. The public's fear of and concern with crime, particularly violent crime, have focused much attention on the criminal justice system and on corrections. Federal court intervention over the past fifteen years has been a significant concern to correctional systems, especially in areas related to classification.

In addition to the information generated for facility and program planning, classification systems can also provide useful information on how effectively a correctional system is performing and meeting established goals. Such information can answer several questions:

1. Is the offender population being classified according to established security and custody objectives?

2. Is the system overclassifying?

3. To what degree are the objective classification criteria being overridden (10 percent of the time, 20 percent)?

4. Are programs being designed and implemented consistent with the needs of offenders or based on other factors, such as staff experience and interest?

5. Has the offender population changed? What changes are projected over the next several years?

Any true process continuously strives to improve itself through feedback, evaluation, and action to correct deficiencies. To be effective, an objective classification system must be able to improve continuously to meet the changing needs of inmates, the correctional system as a whole, and the interests and concerns of the public. It must respond to emerging knowledge, trends, and professional understanding of the classification process. The system must inform and must also respond to feedback from staff and inmates.

Public Safety and Protection

As violent crime and the fear of it have increased, so has the public's concern for safety. The public looks to the correctional system to prevent escapes, to effectively supervise offenders in the community, and to release only those inmates who are capable of refraining from criminal activity. Public concern and pressure may also surface in determinate or mandatory sentences for certain offenses and in resistance to community correctional programs or intermediate sanctions. Although objective classification might not directly affect all these areas, it clearly has a role in allowing corrections to confront the concerns of the general public.

Future Issues in Objective Classification

Although improvements in correctional classification have been made over the past ten to twelve years, a number of critical issues must be confronted to continue making objective classification systems more efficient and more relevant to managers. Although early objective classification systems have proved to be quite valuable, they also have a number of problems and limitations that must be addressed to ensure their continued effectiveness. For instance, most systems have not been evaluated and validated, and many do not reflect a jurisdiction's criminal justice/correctional philosophy. Also, objective systems should be more comprehensive than they have been, taking into consideration factors in addition to those associated with custody and security.

Criminal Justice Policy and Philosophy and Objective Classification Systems

Part of understanding exactly how and how well classification is operating is to understand what its purposes are, because the purposes of classification within institutions do not exist in a vacuum. They are related to the overall criminal justice sentencing structure in the state, the mission of the agency, and the mission of specific institutions. Sanctioning purposes vary greatly from state to state, and it is important to understand the framework in (each) state to determine whether and how the classification system can be as supportive as possible of that orientation (Burke & Adams 1991).

An essential component of the framework for an objective classification system is therefore a policy statement that sets forth the jurisdiction's sanctioning philosophy or policy and the department's goals, objectives, and purposes for the classification system.

Evaluation and Validation of Objective Classification Systems

A recent study concluded that "Despite the obvious need for evaluation, very few 'formal' evaluation studies have been done.... Only 19 jurisdictions had conducted formal studies. Failing to evaluate objective classification systems is to neglect one of the greatest advantages of these systems. One of the potential strengths of objective classification systems is that they are particularly amenable to evaluation" (Alexander & Austin 1992). Evaluation and validation of classification is important to the following:

- providing a detailed description of how the system is functioning

- comparing how the system is functioning with the original design

- determining what effects the system has on key indicators (i.e., assaults, escapes, staff morale, operational costs)

- determining whether an objective system increases the consistency and reliability of the decisions being made

Correctional systems must be able to demonstrate that objective classification systems are objective, logical, and fundamentally fair and have been designed to meet the needs of both the inmate and the correctional system.

Comprehensive Objective Classification Systems

Objective classification systems designed and implemented from the late 1970s to the present primarily stressed security and custody decision making (e.g., screening for risk). Although some of these systems also had the ability to assess offenders' needs for service, the major aim was risk assessment. This emphasis was consistent with the swing toward determinate sentencing and the reemergence of the retributive and incapacitative philosophies growing out of the "nothing works" mentality of the rehabilitation and reintegration philosophies in the 1970s and 1980s. With jurisdictions moderating their philosophies in the 1990s, the current generation of objective classification systems must be capable of going beyond risk assessment. Classification systems must assess offenders and match them with appropriate programs, services, and treatment opportunities. Objective systems must be sensitive to a diverse culture within correctional systems as well as other changing offender characteristics (e.g., different medical needs and various special needs populations).

Gender Issues—Female Offenders

Burke and Adams (1991) note that the central issue in classification as it relates to female offenders is whether current mainstream classification systems provide adequate tools for managing female offenders. They do not—not because better risk assessment instruments are needed, but rather because different approaches to classification for women in general are needed. "Although significant problems have been identified for women offenders as a result of classification systems designed for an all male population, the solution does not lie in the development of classification specifically for women. It is important that gender not be utilized as a classifying principle" (Burke & Adams 1991).

Because female offenders are not generally viewed as a high-risk population, the major emphasis of any objective classification system should be to focus on nonsecurity issues, such as rehabilitation, programming, preparation for release, and appropriate supervision in transition and community correctional programs.

Intermediate Sanctions

U.S. sentencing tradition and practices have overemphasized the importance of the prison and incapacitation and, thus, have failed to fully use alternative short-term incarcerative and nonincarcerative sanctions for nonviolent offenders. For specific groups of offenders, intermediate sanctions are at least as effective as imprisonment and certainly less costly. State correctional systems could expand the use of intermediate sanctions, including such programs as day reporting centers, restitution, split sentences, shock incarceration, home confinement both with and without electronic monitoring, and halfway houses and halfway-back programs. Departments of correction can create a range of sanctions for before and after incarceration to appropriately and effectively meet the offender populations they serve. Objective classification systems can be designed to assess these diverse populations for risk and to place them in appropriate programs. Growing numbers of offenders, increasing correctional costs, and diminishing fiscal resources will continue to make intermediate sanctions viable options.

Conclusion

The contemporary prison classification system began as a subjective decision-making process. The revolution in prison classification that took place in the late 1970s and early 1980s evolved toward objective classification systems that first stressed security and custody issues and subsequently began to balance these considerations with program needs of offenders. It appears that the field of prison classification is now ready to continue this revolution toward classification systems that are validated and evaluated, that express criminal justice philosophies and clearly defined goals and objectives, that are responsive to women and culturally diverse offender differences and needs, and that assist in making more efficient use of a broad range of correctional sanctions and options.

Contemporary prison systems still need to be concerned about public safety, security, and custody, but these concerns must be balanced with classification systems that are sensitive to offender needs for programs, effectively use diminishing resources, and promote the greater use of innovative correctional programs.

References

Alexander, Jack, and James Austin. June 1992. *Handbook for evaluating prison classification systems*. Washington, D.C.: National Institute of Corrections.

Buchanan, Robert A., Karen L. Whitlow, and James Austin. 1986. National evaluation of objective classification system: The current state of the art. *Crime and Delinquency* 32:272–90.

Buchanan, Robert A., and Karen L. Whitlow. June 1987. *Guidelines for developing, implementing, and revising an objective prison classification system*. Washington, D.C.: National Institute of Justice.

Bureau of Justice Statistics. January 1993. *National Update II*, No. 3. Washington, D.C.: Bureau of Justice Statistics.

Burke, Peggy, and Linda Adams. March 1991. *Classification of women offenders in state correctional facilities: A handbook for practitioners*. Washington, D.C.: National Institute of Corrections.

Camp, George M., and Camille Graham Camp. 1991. *The corrections yearbook 1991*. South Salem, N.Y.: Criminal Justice Institute.

Camp, George M., and Camille Graham Camp. 1992. *The corrections yearbook 1992*. South Salem, N.Y.: Criminal Justice Institute.

Clements, Carl B. 1984. *Offender needs assessment: Models and approaches*. Washington, D.C.: National Institute of Justice.

Clements, Carl B. October 1988. The measurement and evaluation of correctional resources management. In *Classification: Innovative correctional programs*. Richmond, Ky.: Department of Criminal Justice, Eastern Kentucky University.

Greenfeld, Lawrence. April 1992. *Prisons and prisoners in the United States*. Washington, D.C.: Bureau of Justice Statistics.

II. Legal Issues in Classification

By Barbara Belbot, J.D., and Rolando V. del Carmen, J.S.D.

S ince courts abandoned the "hands off" doctrine in the mid-1960s, prisons have been awash in litigation. There is hardly an aspect of prison life that has not been litigated in court. That process is ongoing and, although the major contours of prison law have been delineated by court decisions, new issues continue to emerge and old issues refined. One of the concerns that has been addressed by courts over the years is inmate classification.

Courts recognize that although inmates do not have a constitutional right to a classification system, such systems may be necessary to provide inmates their constitutional right to a reasonably safe and secure living environment (*Grubbs v. Bradley*, 552 F. Supp. 1052 [M.D. Tenn. 1982]). Many prison and jail reform lawsuits have led to the implementation or revision of classification schemes to include criteria that clearly establish rational and reasonable grounds for classifying inmates and procedures that mandate the manner in which these criteria are to be implemented.

Classifying inmates concerns more than just assigning security or custody levels. It also includes transferring inmates from one institution to another and assigning them prison jobs and housing.

Decisions by medical and psychiatric providers and disciplinary staff greatly affect the classification process, making it a complex mechanism for managing inmates who have a host of educational, vocational, and programmatic needs. Classification law will continue to

Barbara Belbot, J.D., is a professor of criminal justice at the University of Houston—Downtown and a doctoral fellow at Sam Houston State University in Huntsville, Texas. Rolando V. del Carmen is a professor at the Sam Houston State University Criminal Justice Center in Huntsville.

develop as correctional agencies and courts grapple with the many factors that influence an inmate's classification status.

A study of the decided cases shows five major current legal issues surrounding classification: due process rights afforded inmates during classification, pretrial detainees, classification criteria, failure to protect, and segregating inmates who have tested positive for human immunodeficiency virus (HIV).

Right to Due Process

In *Vitek v. Jones* (445 U.S. 480 [1980]), the Supreme Court mandated that certain procedural safeguards must be afforded inmates faced with transfer from a prison facility to a mental institution. The court said that not only did Nebraska law provide a liberty interest in remaining in a prison setting, the Constitution itself required due process protection prior to such a transfer. Involuntary commitment to a mental health facility entails more serious consequences than the loss of freedom when confined in a penal institution. It may result in social stigma, forced behavior modification treatment, and greater limits on an inmate's freedom. *Vitek* is the only instance in which the Supreme Court gave inmates involved in a transfer or classification decision procedural protections directly afforded by the due process clause of the Fourteenth Amendment. The unique nature of the transfer—involuntary commitment to a mental institution—justified the application of Fourteenth Amendment due process.

In contrast, the Supreme Court and lower federal courts have rejected claims of direct constitutional safeguards for inmates involved in transfer and classification decisions that do not include mental health commitments. Instead, arguments that inmates have been transferred from one facility to another or initially classified or reclassified to a custody status without adequate due process have been analyzed according to the concept of state-created liberty interests.

The concept of state-created liberty interest is best understood as:

> Where the government theoretically has complete discretion in a matter but chooses, through statute, administrative rule, policy or a similar sort of document, to limit its discretion in some way, then the state must follow some sort of procedural steps (due process) to assure that it is making the decision consistent with the limitation it has imposed on itself (ACA 1987).

In short, even if the Constitution itself does not mandate due process, as it did in *Vitek*, due process protections may be triggered by provisions of state law or administrative rule that define when an action, such as an inmate transfer, should take place.

In a case dealing directly with inmate classification issues, *Meachum v. Fano* (427 U.S. 215 [1976]), the Supreme Court distinguished between due process protections that originate in the Constitution and those that are created by state statute. In *Meachum*, several inmates were transferred from a medium-security facility in Norfolk, Massachusetts, to a maximum-security facility in Walpole, Massachusetts, where the living conditions were substantially less favorable than those at Norfolk. The inmates were transferred because they were suspected of setting fires in the institution, although they were never disciplined for those offenses. They alleged that the hearing they were afforded prior to their transfers was constitutionally inadequate. The Supreme Court ruled that the Constitution does not guarantee that an inmate will be placed in any particular prison if a state has more than one facility. The decision to assign an inmate to a particular facility does not initiate due process protection even if life in one prison is more disagreeable than life in another. Neither does the Constitution protect an inmate against transfer from one institution to another within the prison system.

The Supreme Court went on to consider whether Massachusetts law created a liberty interest for inmates to remain in any particular institution. The court decided that Massachusetts law gave prison officials a lot of power to assign and transfer inmates under a wide variety of circumstances and, as worded, did not confer a liberty interest requiring constitutional protection.

Montanye v. Haymes (427 U.S. 236 [1976]) was decided the same day as *Meachum v. Fano*. Haymes was removed from his assignment as an inmate clerk in the law library at the Attica correctional facility in New York. After he circulated a petition among inmates alleging that they were deprived of legal assistance because of his removal, he was transferred to another facility within the state. Prison officials stated that he was removed from his assignment because he violated regulations governing library use. Haymes alleged that he was transferred in retaliation for providing legal assistance to other inmates. The Supreme Court determined that it did not matter why the inmate was transferred because the Constitution's due process clause does not require hearings in connection with transfers, whether they result from an inmate's behavior or are labeled disciplinary or punitive. The court also ruled that New York law did not give Haymes the right to remain at a particular institution.

In *Hewitt v. Helms* (459 U.S. 460 [1983]), the Supreme Court outlined in greater detail the current law of state-created liberty interests in prison regulations, statutes, and polices. Inmate Helms was removed from the general population and placed in administrative segregation following a riot in a Pennsylvania prison facility. Although he was absolved of misconduct five days after his transfer, the hearing committee ordered that he remain in administrative segregation because he was a threat to other inmates. Criminal charges were filed against him three days later. Three weeks later, a committee of prison staff reviewed his administrative segregation placement and concluded he should remain assigned there until further proceedings. Based on a second misconduct report, he was found guilty and confined to administrative segregation for six months. Helms argued that the informal procedures afforded him were constitutionally inadequate and that he had been held in segregated status without proper safeguards.

The Supreme Court analyzed Helms's claim by identifying two possible sources of liberty interests: the due process clause itself and state law. The court rejected the argument that the Constitution provided Helms a liberty interest in remaining in the general population. Prison administrators require broad discretion in managing inmates, and respect must be paid to their decisions. As long as the conditions of confinement are constitutional and within the sentence imposed, due process is not violated. Moreover, administrative segregation is something every inmate can expect to face at some point during incarceration and this was within the term of Helms's sentence.

The court ruled, however, that the state had created a liberty interest by enacting statutes and regulations governing the use of administrative segregation that restricted the discretion of prison officials. The state went beyond simple procedural guidelines by using explicit mandatory language requiring that certain procedures "shall," "will," and "must" be employed. The regulations also provided that placement in administrative segregation would not occur in the absence of legal justifications, such as the need for control or threat of a serious disturbance. Nonetheless, the court concluded that considering what was at stake for both the institution and the inmate when assigning an inmate to administrative segregation, the informal, nonadversarial procedures provided by the regulations and afforded Helms were adequate to protect his state-created liberty interest.

Several months later in 1983, the Supreme Court decided another case involving the transfer of an inmate. In *Olim v. Wakinekona* (461 U.S. 238 [1983]), an inmate of the Hawaii State Prison was transferred to a mainland facility. Wakinekona argued that there were procedural ir-regularities in his transfer and that his constitutional right to due process had been violated. The Supreme Court disagreed. Relying on *Meachum v. Fano* and *Montanye v. Haymes*, which dealt with intrastate transfers, the court concluded that an inmate has no justifiable expectation that he will be incarcerated in a facility in any particular state. Wakinekona, therefore, did not have a liberty interest protected directly by the Constitution. Fur-thermore, the state had not created a liberty interest because Hawaii's rules did not place substantive limitations on official discretion to decide which inmates should be transferred. In addition, the court concluded that the regulations did not require a particular kind of hearing prior to trans-fer.

Numerous decisions by lower federal courts have examined inmate classification decisions in light of *Meachum v. Fano*, *Montayne v. Haymes*, *Hewitt v. Helms*, and *Olim v. Wakinekona*. The courts have had to review state statutes, regulations, and policies to determine whether they create a liberty interest that activates due process protections and, if so, whether those protections were adequately provided. There are a myriad of different fact situations in the lower court cases that are as numerous as the cases themselves.

In *Miller v. Henman* (804 F.2d 421 [7th Cir. 1986]), a federal inmate transferred to the Marion maximum security facility, the most secure and only level 6 prison in the federal prison system, argued that conditions at Marion were so different from other federal prisons that he was entitled to a due process hearing prior to his transfer. In addition, federal regulations governing security classification establish a legitimate claim of entitle-ment to one classification over another. As a level 5 security classifica-tion, he argued he should not be held in a level 6 facility because he was not found suitable for the facility pursuant to the Bureau of Prisons' own written policies.

The Seventh Circuit Court of Appeals rejected Miller's arguments. Marion does not provide a punishment that is so different from what is characteristically suffered by a convicted offender. Furthermore, the Bureau of Prisons regulations addressing classification and assign-ment/transfer decisions are not binding regulations that limit the discretion of the decision maker. Miller had no constitutionally protected right to due process before he was transferred to Marion.

Frank Castaneda also challenged his transfer to Marion in *Cas-taneda v. Henman* (48 CrL 1080 [7th Cir. 1990]). He alleged that his transfer was based on false information in his inmate file that he was a gang member, involved in extortion for sex, and a known killer. He claimed that the transfer was for disciplinary reasons, which entitled him to a due process hearing. Bureau regulations set out specific criteria for transferring an inmate from one prison to another for disciplinary reasons. The Seventh Circuit Court of Appeals, however, found that the regulations established no criteria for administrative transfers. Absent criteria, and recognizing that there may exist multiple reasons for transferring an inmate, a hearing was not required.

The Third Circuit denied relief to an inmate who argued that he was not afforded due process before he was transferred to administrative segregation for two months (*Stephany v. Wagner*, 835 F.2d 497 [3rd Cir.1986]). Stephany was never provided a hearing, but his transfer and assignment were reviewed regularly over the two-month period. He was never charged with misconduct. Although the institution's inmate handbook listed specific situations for which placement in administrative segregation was appropriate, the court ruled that the criteria listed did not limit official discretion because, unlike *Hewitt v. Helms*, it did not have explicitly mandatory language. The regulations did not use words like "will," "shall," or "must" in directing prison administrators.

The inmate-plaintiff in *Beard v. Livesay* (798 F.2d 874 [6th Cir.1986]) was more successful than Stephany. Beard argued that Tennessee statutes and regulations required that he be given a hearing prior to his reclassification from minimum to maximum security. The Federal Court of Appeals agreed that the language of the regulations was mandatory in nature, adopting an elaborate scheme for reclassification that limited official discretion and required a due process hearing. The court clearly noted that a protected liberty interest can be created pursuant to agency and departmental rules and regulations and not just state statutory law.

In *Madewell v. Roberts* (909 F.2d 1203 [8th Cir. 1990]), inmates argued that because of their partial medical disability, prison regulations prevented them from performing the types of jobs that would allow them to achieve the highest class I classification status. The court dismissed the argument that inmates have a liberty interest in a particular class status. It noted, however, that while an inmate's medical condition can be rationally related to his job assignment, his medical condition may be an arbitrary factor for determining his class status, in violation of the Fourteenth Amendment's equal protection clause. The court remanded the case for further consideration.

In another case, inmate Smith was transferred from a medium to a maximum security prison in Massachusetts. He was eventually found guilty of engaging in unauthorized sex with another inmate and reclassified to maximum security for one year. The Federal Appeals Court in *Smith v. Massachusetts Department of Corrections* (936 F.2d 1390 [1st Cir. 1991]), considered a classification contract that Smith had agreed to several years before with the corrections agency. It provided that Smith would be transferred to successively less restrictive facilities on the successful completion of certain programs and job training. A positive urinalysis or a major disciplinary report could result in a renegotiation of the contract. Smith alleged that not only state regulations but also his contract with the agency required he be given notice and a hearing prior to transfer. The court ruled that neither state law nor the contract established substantive limitations on the discretion of officials to transfer or reclassify an inmate.

The appellate court distinguished Smith's case from *Lanier v. Fair* (876 F.2d 243 [1st Cir. 1989]). In *Lanier*, the court held that Massachusetts procedures governing inmate transfers from halfway houses together with a community release agreement gave inmates a protected liberty interest in remaining in a halfway house. The correctional department's regulations did not create substantive limitations, but the program guidelines concerning the operation of the community centers indicated that a return to a more restrictive facility could only occur when an inmate had violated certain regulations. In addition, the community release agreement signed by the inmates gave them a legitimate expectation that they would be returned only for violating established rules.

An Illinois prison regulation requires officials to follow certain procedures before transferring or removing an inmate from a job assignment for disciplinary reasons. No other types of work assignments, however, require a due process hearing. In *Wallace v. Robinson* (940 F.2d 243 [7th Cir. 1991]), the Seventh Circuit Court of Appeals considered a claim by an inmate that he was transferred to a lower paying job for disciplinary reasons, although the administration claimed he had poor work habits. Based on agency rules, the court concluded that an inmate can be removed from a job for any reason or no reason at all without any sort of procedure, as long as the justification is not disciplinary.

To summarize, whether a correctional department is affording adequate due process to inmates in the transfer or classification process will depend on the language of state law and the agency's regulations. There are no hard and fast rules, and courts will make decisions on a case-by-case basis, relying primarily on how the statute or regulation is worded. If the statute or regulation sets forth "specific substantive predicates," a set of criteria establishing under what circumstances an inmate can be transferred, classified, or reclassified, a liberty interest still has not been created unless the language of the law explicitly mandates that officials "must," "shall," or "will" take certain steps under those circumstances. Terms such as "may" or "can" do not limit administrative discretion and tend not to create liberty interests. If laws or regulations provide specific criteria or procedures in mandatory form, it is likely that a reviewing court will find the state has created a liberty interest. If such an interest exists, an agency must provide inmates adequate due process in the form of notice and hearing to make certain the agency abides by the limitations set forth in its own criteria and procedures.

Pretrial Detainees

The dominant legal issue related to classification and pretrial detainees concerns the failure to protect detainees from other detainees or from convicted offenders with whom they are often housed. Because they are not convicted, pretrial detainees are not protected by the Eighth Amendment (*Bell v. Wolfish*, 441 U.S. 520 [1979]); however, courts regularly apply the Fifth and Fourteenth Amendments' due process clauses so as to give detainees the same measure of protection (*Berry v. City of Muskogee*, 900 F.2d 1489 [10th Cir. 1990]).

Several courts have ruled that pretrial detainees should not be housed in the same cell or cellblock as convicted offenders (*Alberti v. Sheriff of Harris County*, 406 F.Supp. 649 [S.D. Tex. 1975]). Other courts have ruled that there is no inherent constitutional violation in failing to separate sentenced and pretrial inmates, although detainees have a right to be housed separately from known convicted offenders who may threaten their safety (*Campbell v. Bergeron*, 486 F.Supp. 1246 [M.D. La. 1980]; *Ryan v. Burlington County*, 860 F.2d 1199 [3rd Cir. 1988]). Jail administrators can expect that failing to separate the two types of inmates will be a major factor in a detainee's claim that he or she was injured by a sentenced inmate, as it was in *Ryan v. Burlington County* (708 F.Supp. 623 [D. N.J. 1989]), which found a jail captain and warden liable for failing to institute a classification system separating pretrial inmates from dangerous, convicted offenders.

Classification Criteria

Courts have held that in general classification criteria must be rational and reasonable as opposed to arbitrary and capricious (*Kelley v. Brewer*, 525 F.2d 394 [8th Cir. 1975]; *Laaman v. Helgemoe*, 437 F.Supp. 269 [D. N.H. 1977]). In addition, prison officials cannot reclassify an inmate or transfer his or her job assignment in retaliation for the exercise of a constitutional right, such as filing lawsuits and grievances, or exercising a First Amendment right in a way that does not adversely affect a legitimate state interest (*Jackson v. Cain*, 864 F.2d 1235 [5th Cir. 1989]; *Madewell v. Roberts* [1990]).

The Fourteenth Amendment's equal protection clause prohibits racial discrimination within prisons and jails, including the segregation of inmates. Authorities acting in good faith and in particularized circumstances are permitted, however, to take into account racial tensions in maintaining security, discipline, and good order in prisons and jails (*Lee v. Washington*, 390 U.S. 333 [1968]). Such consideration should be made after a danger to security, discipline, and good order has become apparent and not before (*Wilson v. Kelley*, 294 F.Supp. 1005 [N.D. Ga. 1968]). Inmates are also protected from racial discrimination in job assignments, but an inmate does not have a constitutional right to any particular job status (*Terrell v. State of Mississippi*, 573 So.2d 732 [Miss. 1990]).

Classification policies that deny sex offenders minimum security status and participation in certain programs, such as work release and furloughs, have been held constitutional against allegations that they violate the equal protection clause of the Constitution (*Hendking v. Smith*, 781 F.2d 850 [11th Cir. 1986]; *Monroe v. Thigpen*, 932 F.2d 1437 [11th Cir. 1991]).

Failure to Protect

In *DeShaney v. Winnebago County Department of Social Services* (489 U.S. 189 [1989]), the Supreme Court held that the state has no duty to protect individuals who are not in state custody, adding that

> When the State takes a person into its custody and holds him there against his will, the Constitution imposes upon it a corresponding duty to assume some responsibility for his safety and general well-being.

Lower federal courts have recognized that based on the Eighth Amendment's prohibition against cruel and unusual punishment, inmates have a constitutional right to reasonable protection from violence and sexual assault perpetrated by fellow inmates. In *Woodhous v. Virginia* (487 F.2d 889 [4th Cir. 1973]), the Fourth Circuit Court of Appeals ruled that an inmate can sustain a lawsuit if he proves a pervasive risk of harm from other inmates to which officials failed to reasonably respond. In a later case, *Withers v. Levine* (615 F.2d 158 [4th Cir.1980]), the same court held that it is enough that violence and sexual assaults occur with sufficient frequency that inmates are put in reasonable fear for their safety and reasonably apprise officials of the problem and their need for protection.

Although many failure-to-protect lawsuits do not involve transfer or classification issues, some do. In *Martin v. White* (742 F.2d 469 [8th Cir.1984]), the Eighth Circuit Court of Appeals considered allegations that the administration failed to provide inmates protection from the threat of rape. Included in their claims was a failure to classify inmates according to their violent histories. The trial court granted the state's motion for a directed verdict, effectively dismissing the inmates' case. The appellate court, however, reversed and remanded, holding that a pervasive risk of harm was established and that officials should have the opportunity to show if they reasonably responded to it.

A jail inmate in *Morgan v. District of Columbia* (824 F.2d 1049 [D.C. Cir. 1987]) alleged that because of severe crowding he was assigned to a bunk in a dayroom converted into a dormitory to accommodate the overflow of inmates. Morgan sustained serious eye injuries after an assault by a fellow inmate who had psychiatric problems and a history of physical violence. The District of Columbia Court of Appeals upheld the jury's decision finding that the District was deliberately indifferent to Morgan's safety. Officials knew of the attacker's psychiatric problems and history of violence and failed to place him in a more secure setting.

In *Walsh v. Mellas* (837 F.2d 789 [7th Cir. 1988]), an inmate was injured by a gang member assigned to his cell. The Seventh Circuit Court of Appeals concluded that there was sufficient evidence that officials failed to use reasonable screening procedures and safeguards to protect the safety of inmates from gang-related violence. The court emphasized that a good faith procedure for reviewing an inmate's file before assigning him or her a cell or work partner would have likely revealed a gang-related history, which would have helped insulate officials from a finding that their classification procedures were unconstitutional.

In *Roland v. Johnson* (856 F.2d 764 [6th Cir. 1988]), the Sixth Circuit Court of Appeals decided that the inmate-plaintiff had presented genuine issues of material fact when he alleged he was attacked by inmates housed in his medium custody cellblock, but who were actually close custody status and who had job assignments that allowed them to operate mechanical devices to open the cells of other inmates. The matter was sent back to the trial court. The First Circuit also remanded a case to the trial court for further consideration in *Cortes-Quinones v. Jiminez-Nettleship* (842 F.2d 556 [1st Cir. 1988]). The mother of a psychiatrically disturbed inmate alleged her son was murdered by other inmates when officials failed to place him in a more secure setting.

The Ninth Circuit ruled in *Redman v. San Diego County* (942 F.2d 1435 [4th Cir. 1991]), that there was sufficient evidence that jail administrators were deliberately indifferent to plaintiff's security because of a policy to place aggressive homosexuals in the general population while isolating passive homosexuals. The plaintiff was raped several times by fellow inmates.

A 1992 decision by the Sixth Circuit Court of Appeals, *Doe v. Sullivan County* (956 F.2d 545 [6th Cir. 1992]), considered a sexual assault on a young, mentally handicapped jail inmate assigned to general population. The court found that the county's regulations concerning inmate classification included explicitly mandatory language that limited official discretion in classifying violent, homosexual, vulnerable, and mentally handicapped inmates. The injured inmate had a state-created liberty interest in a safe classification.

Although courts have recognized that inmates have an Eighth Amendment right to reasonable protection from other inmates, there is substantial disagreement among the Courts of Appeal concerning the proper legal standard to evaluate the constitutional claim. Courts agree that to be held liable, prison officials must have been deliberately indifferent to the risk of injury to an inmate. The difficulty is interpreting the meaning of "deliberate indifference."

Estelle v. Gamble (429 U.S. 97 [1976]) is clear that deliberate indifference entails more than a lack of ordinary care or negligence. In that seminal case, the Supreme Court said that "unnecessary and wanton" infliction of pain constitutes deliberate indifference, which, in turn, violates the Eighth Amendment. In 1986, the Supreme Court decided that prison officials responsible for shooting an inmate during a riot were liable only on a showing that they acted maliciously and sadistically (*Whitley v. Albers*, 475 U.S. 312 [1986]). In *Hudson v. McMillian* (112 U.S. 995 [1992]), the Court held that the use of excessive force against an inmate may constitute cruel and unusual punishment even if the inmate is not seriously injured.

Several appellate courts have applied the *Whitley v. Albers* interpretation to failure-to-protect claims, arguing that *Whitley* should not be confined to prison riots. In those circuits, inmates must prove that officials intended them harm or had actual knowledge that a dangerous situation existed (*McGill v. Duckworth*, 994 F.2d 344 [7th Cir. 1991]; *Moore v. Winebrenner*, 927 F.2d 1312 [4th Cir. 1991]). Other circuits have held that the malicious indifference standard is not applicable to failure-to-protect claims and that deliberate indifference as interpreted by *Estelle* is the appropriate inquiry (*Berry v. City of Muskogee* [1990], *Redman v. San Diego County* [1991]).

In addition to potential liability for the denial of an inmate's constitutional rights, administrators face the possibility of being found liable under a state's personal injury law. Tort law requires correctional officials to use reasonable care to ensure the safety of inmates during incarceration, including protecting them from other inmates. Unlike constitutional claims, ordinary negligence suffices in state tort cases, but plaintiffs usually must show that officials had actual or constructive notice of the danger, meaning they knew or had reason to know about a dangerous situation (*Saunders v. State*, 446 A.2d 748 [R.I. 1982]; *Department of Health and Rehabilitative Services v. Whaley*, 574 So.2d 100 [Fla. 1991]).

Correctional agencies should expect a fair amount of failure-to-protect litigation. In a prison or jail environment there will be numerous circumstances that can generate such claims. Classification issues play a major role in many of these lawsuits, usually combined with other allegations, such as insufficient supervision and unsafe facilities. Prison crowding also creates troublesome classification issues. A well-operated, responsive classification system can be an important defense. Agencies that regularly review inmate classifications, update files to reflect current information, and assign inmates to housing and jobs that are appropriate for their custody and security levels will curtail their legal losses as well as violence in their institutions.

HIV-positive Inmates

Some states have statutes that specifically allow for the segregation of inmates with acquired immunodeficiency syndrome (AIDS). Several federal courts have decided that segregating inmates who are HIV-positive does not violate the Eighth Amendment prohibition against cruel and unusual punishment nor does it violate the equal protection clause (*Cordero v. Coughlin*, 607 F.Supp. 9 [S.D. N.Y. 1984]; *Harris v. Thigpen*, 941 F.2d 1495 [11th Cir. 1991]). Only two courts have ruled that segregation does present constitutional problems because it advertises the inmates' medical conditions in violation of their constitutional right to privacy (*Doe v. Coughlin*, 696 F.Supp. 1234 [N.D. N.Y. 1988]; *Nolley v. Erie County*, 776 F.Supp. 715 [W.D. N.Y. 1991]). A federal appellate court has ruled that the failure to segregate HIV-positive inmates does not violate the Eighth Amendment rights of noninfected inmates (*Robbins v. Clarke*, 946 F.2d 1331 [8th Cir. 1991]).

Currently, with few exceptions, prison administrators are free from constitutional restraints to segregate or not segregate inmates with AIDS. Section 504 of the Rehabilitation Act, however, may present some constraints on their discretion. Although a district court in Wisconsin upheld the Federal Bureau of Prison's policy that prohibits all inmates with HIV from working in prison hospitals or food services (*Farmer v. Moritsugu*, 742 F.Supp. 525 [W.D. Wisc. 1990]), an Arizona federal court ruled that such blanket prohibitions are prohibited under section 504. According to that court, officials must show that an individual inmate with HIV would present a significant risk of transmitting the virus if he or she worked in food services and that no reasonable accommodation would reduce the risk to a significant level (*Casey v. Lewis*, 773 F.Supp. 1365 [D. Ariz. 1991]). The *Harris v. Thigpen* (1991) court ruled that officials must make a similar showing under section 504 before prohibiting inmates with AIDS to participate in various prison programs and activities.

Summary and Conclusion

Classification systems and individual classification decisions can be the subject of a number of legal challenges. Prison administrators should expect that as courts resolve one legal issue involving classification, another issue will develop because of the nature of the process. There are too many situations that can never be fully anticipated, and legal issues continue to unfold. Correctional officials, however, can learn from the court cases that have already been decided.

To begin, officials can control the manner in which classification criteria and procedures are designed. Administrators should pay attention during the drafting process to the potential legal ramifications that may result from a particular system. Different agencies will prefer to deal with different legal issues. Reducing official discretion may be attractive to departments that would prefer uniform application of criteria and procedures and a consequent reduction in arbitrary decision making. Another department may choose to allow for more discretion to avoid the structure (forms, hearings, and the personnel to attend to them) that limited discretion imposes. Different types of classification decisions (e.g., assigning custody levels versus intrastate transfers) may be better served by different types of schemes. Jail administrators must be especially aware of the need to separate dangerous, convicted offenders from pretrial detainees. Current case law generally permits the segregation of HIV-positive inmates, as do many state statutes; however, section 504 of the Rehabilitation Act may limit officials from prohibiting inmates with HIV from participating in jobs and prison programs.

Officials must remember that a statute or regulation that lists a set of criteria establishing under what circumstances an inmate may be transferred, classified, or reclassified creates a liberty interest if, in addition, the language of the law or regulation explicitly mandates that officials "must," "shall," or "will" take certain steps under those circumstances.

Officials can also control the manner in which a classification scheme is administered. If a state has created a liberty interest, administrative discretion is limited, and individual decisions must carefully abide by established criteria and procedures. Agency personnel are obligated under the law to provide inmates adequate due process in the form of notice and hearing. Even if a state has not created a liberty interest, classification cannot be used to retaliate against an inmate exercising his or her constitutional rights or to discriminate based on race.

Classification constitutes the nerve center of inmate management. It will become an increasingly complicated process as it responds to issues raised by inmates with special needs. Crowded facilities will only aggravate complications. A well-operated system for classifying inmates in a facility that then assigns them to appropriate housing and job categories will not only reduce inmate-on-inmate violence, but will also act as proof in a failure-to-protect lawsuit that officials were not deliberately indifferent to an inmate's needs. Administrators should realize that classification is one of their best tools to avoid lawsuits and, if that is not possible, one of their best defenses.

Reference

American Correctional Association. 1987. *Legal Responsibility and Authority of Correctional Officers: A Handbook on Courts, Judicial Decisions and Constitutional Requirements.* College Park, Md.: ACA.

III. Classification: The Role of Upper Management

by James E. Aiken

Correctional administrators often find themselves trying to balance the value of a classification system between the expectations of two groups: the public, which expects correctional agencies to protect and reassure it, and corrections, which needs to follow sound correctional practice based on realistic resources, constraints, and expectations.

The daily experiences of many administrators underscore the diversity of the two groups. The classification system may also be affected by the demands and expectations of the two groups. Sometimes the public demands changes to classification systems overnight. A tragic incident may lead to classification criteria changes, and the inmate population may be moved to accommodate the expectations of the public or corrections.

Correctional administrators should resist allowing a single major event, such as a riot or a crime committed in the community by an inmate, to dictate their agency's classification practices. The agency's classification system should be kept in place even during critical periods. This is not to say that classification systems should not be flexible. Rather, changes should be made based on research, planning, and quantifiable data and not in response to stressful and emotional events.

Some staff may feel the classification system deprives them of the flexibility they need to place inmates in available bed space. This is especially true when crowded conditions and court-ordered caps are in place. Staff may feel that the classification system does not truly reflect the operational or programmatic needs of the agency. Administrators often make quick decisions regarding the value of classification, leaving staff in a state of discord.

It is important to set the value of a classification system. This can be done by studying the public and corrections for a common ground for the

---

James E. Aiken is director of the Bureau of Corrections in the U.S. Virgin Islands.

32

system to operate. It focuses decision-making priorities and policies. The foundation of a classification system should be based on what the agency determines will benefit both groups. Administrators should facilitate a review of the values of the public and corrections and establish a true value or foundation based on expectations and sound correctional principles.

The following are some examples of values that can be created for classification systems:

1. Public safety is the primary consideration in all decision making regarding inmate classification, including programming and housing assignments.

2. The classification system's primary function is to manage population by identifying the nature of, and providing solutions to, crowding.

3. The primary consideration of the classification system is to manage the day-to-day activities of the correctional system to ensure cost-effective use of bed space, staff, and program resources.

The purpose of identifying classification missions is to transform them into values, to change the written word in policy manuals sitting on shelves to values most people in the organization understand and accept.

Establishing the Process

Once the value for classification is created or recreated, it must be made into a process that will be accepted and understood by both the public and corrections. Many administrators learn that writing memos or holding staff meetings alone do not generate the energy needed to transform a mission into a value.

The question is, how do we communicate words to key stakeholders that demonstrate desired behavior? Many well-meaning and thought-out mission statements have just remained on paper while others have developed into a spirit and practice in which the public and corrections have taken pride and ownership.

Some administrators have even hired consultants to come into their agencies to evaluate needs, establish systems, and train staff. The product has sometimes not met well with the expectations of the organization. The problem often is not with the written words provided by consultants. The problem may be resistance from the public or corrections to "buy-in" and cooperate to create the classification system for mutual benefit.

The following are keys to establishing and maintaining a successful classification system.

Information—Sharing and receiving information regarding the public's and corrections' expectations and values of classification systems help to (1) better focus the issues and the value to be created, (2) create an increased opportunity for a buy-in from staff and other key stakeholders, and (3) serve as an early warning system for identifying potential barriers.

Organization—The development of a methodical management process involving a number of people within the agency and the community for problem-solving and decision-making activities reduces discord, sets priorities, and increases the likelihood of informed decision making.

The organizational makeup must effectively encompass all groups. The energy needed to effect desired change is affected by exclusion of one or more groups, whether or not the exclusion was intended. For example, a classification system that works well with male inmates will not necessarily have the same success with female inmates.

Integrity—Once the value has been created and the classification process implemented, the role of top management is to maintain the priority of the system. Many have found this aspect to be difficult to do, especially when a powerful person requests a movement of inmates that violates the dictates of the system.

Administrators are often reminded that every action they take creates a value or impression. When exceptions are made regarding the classification system, it often sends the message that the value is being reduced to "just a sentence in a policy manual." When this practice continues, the probability increases of a major incident that may cause the administrator and his or her organization undue criticism and embarrassment.

This does not mean that once a classification system is in operation, it should not be changed. Rather, the classification system should reflect the new values generated from the public and corrections.

Communicating Information

Many classification systems use data that are essential for creating sound public policy regarding correctional matters. Sometimes these data are not properly translated into information that could be provided at the right moment to enhance rational approaches to complex correctional issues.

Unfortunately, information that might affect the outcome of a law is often not known until correctional budgets or operations are affected. Administrators may not realize the importance of such information or the information may not be accessible at the time needed. An effort must be made to find out the information prior to the need for it.

Another aspect of communicating information centers around educating the public. The general public does not know who is in prison and why. The information used and generated by the classification system can provide this information about corrections to the public.

It can also place administrators in the role of "information provider," rather than advocates of one position over another. Administrators can then take the position of "standing on high ground" on sensitive issues because they are simply reporting facts that normally are not challenged as to bias.

Summary

The following is a summary of suggestions to help correctional administrators manage their classification systems:

1. Set the value for classification—create or recreate the usefulness of classification by establishing its value based on the public's and corrections' expectations and needs.

2. Establish the process—translate the classification system's value into practice.

3. Maintain the integrity of the classification system—demonstrate behavior that reflects the values of the classification system, and encourage change through a specific process and not through vague exceptions.

4. Communicate information—use the wealth of information used and generated by classification systems to help develop and support sound, rational correctional policy.

Correctional administrators know that satisfying the needs and expectations in terms of inmate classification of both the public and corrections is a difficult task. To do so, administrators need to find a common ground between the two groups and stand firm. The agency's classification system should be based on values that can be translated into a process. Although the process must be championed by the administrator, correctional staff, and the public, all must be open to change that is supported by new information and changing needs.

IV. What Classification for Women?

By Lorraine T. Fowler, Ph.D.

> Prisons for women are the symbolic backwaters of the correctional stream. Separate institutions for women have a shorter history than men's prisons in America. [Despite recent increases] [women] are [still] few in number and small in inmate population size, in part a reflection of the [relative] lack of female involvement in criminal behavior.... A major dilemma facing women inmates is that there has never been enough of them.... An economy of scale has been used to justify fewer services and programs.... Even more important is....sexism.... Institutional work replaced education and viable job training for the labor market after release...."purity, piety, domesticity, and submissiveness"....
>
> This philosophy continues to dominate most women's institutions today....(Hawkins & Alpert 1989).

Four recent publications—two published by the National Institute of Corrections (NIC) and two by the American Correctional Association (ACA)—are both encouraging and disheartening to corrections professionals (ACA 1990; ACA 1993; Brown, Nesbitt & Argento 1984; Burke & Adams 1991). That such influential groups are publishing material on female offenders is a tribute to those organizations and to the capable (and courageous) contributors to these texts.

On the other hand, the tone of the subtitles of these publications— *What Does the Future Hold?*, *Meeting Needs of a Neglected Population*, *An Examination of the Issues*, and *A Handbook for Practitioners*—

Lorraine T. Fowler, Ph.D., is director of Resource and Information Management for the South Carolina Department of Corrections.

suggests that we are far from solving our centuries-old problems related to serving either female offenders or their communities.

"The Sky is Falling"

Kline (ACA 1993) cites the Bureau of Justice Statistics in saying that among state prison populations, the proportion of female offenders in 1991 was 5.6 percent: "The rate of growth for the number of female inmates in state facilities exceeded that for males in each year since 1981. From 1980 to 1989, the male population increased by 112 percent, while the female population increased by 202 percent." However, these numbers translate into 36,921 female inmates as compared with 621,285 male inmates, and again, the proportion of female inmates to male inmates among state prison populations is 5.6 percent as compared with 94.4 percent.

Further, while demographic characteristics between male and female state inmates are very similar—ages cluster between eighteen and forty-five; 39 percent are white non-Hispanic, 12 percent Hispanic, 2.5 percent other, and 46 percent black non-Hispanic—criminal history is different (Kline 1993). According to the Justice Statistics Clearinghouse, almost two-thirds of state female inmates have committed property, drug, or "public order" offenses (59.3 percent), while fewer than half of state male inmates have as "most serious offense" a nonviolent crime (44.8 percent) .

In short, while numbers of female inmates have increased, thereby stressing already inadequate state-level resources for women, total percentage increase at state levels has been between 1.5 percent and 2 percent. Thus, very little has, in fact, changed except that the persistent historical problems of women in corrections have been exacerbated not only by the increase in the numbers but also by the "sky-is-falling" publicity about those numbers. The following facts remain true in state jurisdictions (ACA 1990):

1. There are proportionately fewer female offenders than male offenders.

2. These female offenders are less violent as compared with male offenders (both inside and outside confinement).

3. More than half these women claim children, and most want to keep in touch with them.

4. Poverty, neglect, abuse, emotional problems, drug and alcohol

abuse, poor physical health, little education, and low-skill employment or unemployment continue to be even more characteristic of state female inmates than of comparable male inmates.

5. Programs available to female offenders still concentrate on low-paying traditionally female jobs, such as sewing, cleaning, food service, and cosmetology.

6. Overclassification "over-secures" female offenders, makes them even more dependent and dysfunctional, and does nothing positive to prepare them for work in the community or for being an adequate, functioning parent.

Parity

According to Marjorie Van Ochten (ACA 1993) of the Michigan Department of Corrections Office of Policy and Hearings, "'Separate but equal' is permissible" in prisons. Since 1979, Michigan's Department of Corrections has dealt with the issue of parity thus defined, and it has, in effect, agreed to provide, after many years of arduous litigation, better access to "rehabilitation" opportunities for female inmates and to provide more qualitative programs (e.g., commercial cooking training, as available to men, rather than noncommercial short-order training previously available to women). Special concerns of the court have involved enhanced two-year college programs, nonsexist, "nontraditional" vocational training, apprenticeships, law library access, equal inmate wages, and equal access to a camp program. Van Ochten mentions Connecticut, California, Wisconsin, and Idaho as states that have been responsive without trial to women's constitutional right to due process and equal protection in the matters of at least educational and vocational rehabilitation opportunities. However, she also mentions that parity as defined by case law in this matter does allow for women and men to be separately housed (ACA 1993).

Special problems have been created historically because the comparatively small numbers of women in state jurisdictions are generally placed in one institution. That facility, then, must house the 30 to 40 percent of the female population designated violent, with attendant physical and architectural restraints/constraints that may well prove difficult to avoid for the (majority) nonviolent female offenders. This is an even greater problem than it appears:

The female offender has often been housed in facilities designed for the male population. This is changing, but slowly. Female offenders are given lower priority for resources since their numbers are small compared to the male population. The population explosion continues to divert attention from the female offender as bed space is obtained for a male population boom that although not greater proportionately, is greater in numbers (ACA 1990).

If, as is almost universally the case, designs for men's facilities are used to house women without regard either to "softer" overall criminal history characteristics of women or to lower escape/violence rates or to "special" visitation needs with children, what function can be served by even the most objective, research-based classification system? In short, why bother with classification of women at all?

Existing Classification Systems for Women at State Prisons

Classification is seen as the most effective management tool in corrections, and its misuse is most often blamed when operational problems exist. There is a belief by many practitioners that classification issues are very different for women; a lower percentage of women require close custody and supervision and are less of a threat to each other, staff, or property. Yet, in [our] survey, only 24 percent of state facilities and 26 percent of jails recognize those differences and use specific systems for women. That number is not surprising for local facilities, since the length of stay [is] normally quite short; it is, however, very significant for state facilities (ACA 1990).

Given how every study—recent as well as past—characterizes the "average" female offender as most probably minority, twenty-five to twenty-nine years old, a single parent with one to three children (62 percent), likely a victim of physical and/or sexual abuse as a child, an alcohol and other drug user since age thirteen to fourteen, arrested two to nine times beginning at age fifteen (less than 25 percent for crimes of violence), a high school drop-out, and having received welfare assistance (60 percent) and/or having worked at low-skill clerical or service jobs paying $3.36 to $6.50 an hour (48 percent) (ACA 1990), there is an issue not only of parity rights of female offenders but of the rights of citizens/taxpayers to see cost-effective justice done in their communities.

A study regarding gender equity in classifying male and female offenders by the Massachusetts Probation System makes several critical points worth pursuing by any state-level jurisdiction (Pierce et al. 1991). First, certain indicators of recidivism risk for probationers work well for both men and women: age at first offense; prior record in the past five years; prior probations in the past five years; frequent residency changes; consistent, stable employment; substance abuse problems; "attitude"; and "family structure."

Second, this study found that use of classification forms developed from recidivism prediction analyses that employed the entire caseload of the department, including the small proportion of women, did not discriminate against women placed in maximum probation supervision. Thus, this system that "absorbs" individuals as if they were genderless ("gender neutral"), does indeed produce equity at the highest levels of risk, those about which the community should be most concerned. Preliminary analyses in South Carolina suggest the same phenomenon is operative within institutions as well: gender-neutral instruments sort inmates into higher risk categories similarly, with little regard for gender. Hypothetically, maximum risks are more similar—in prison or in community—in criminal history predictors than they are different in such "soft" variables as family structure, which the Massachusetts study found three times as significant a probation predictor for women as for men.

This leads to the third critical point: use of gender-neutral instruments in Massachusetts was found to result in bias against women placed in moderate or minimum supervision; men were significantly more likely to recidivate than women. An inference drawn in the study that makes sense to corrections practitioners is that these male/female differences are probably due to the finding that women score higher than men on social and economic risk factors, factors less associated with risk of recidivism than are criminal history factors:

> Men sentenced to probation tend to have longer and more substantial prior involvement in the criminal justice system while women are somewhat more likely to have employment and family difficulties.... [W]hile both men and women need employment assistance and family support and substance abuse treatment, women are more likely to need additional support services for their family responsibilities.

[Even more critical,] differences between men and women on probation in Massachusetts may reflect differing expectations and opportunities provided to men and women in general in our society. Chief among potential explanations for these differences is that women typically have the primary or sole responsibility for raising children.... Other factors that may help account for male/female differences include potential unequal treatment of women in terms of employment and/or job training opportunities (Pierce et al. 1991).

Why concentrate on the Massachusetts probation study when the subject under discussion is state-level prison classification for female offenders? Because identical problems exist even in those few prison systems that have thought about accommodating women as a "special class" (with the possible exception of Wyoming's unique internal, behavioral-based system, very different from either clinical judgment systems or empirical risk systems): New York, South Carolina, Illinois.

Current Classification Practice Does Not Work for Female Offenders

Burke and Adams (1991) focus on the issue at hand for jurisdictions struggling with parity or gender equity: systems and facilities intended to house a majority of men and a minority of women with serious criminal histories are probably overclassifying the majority of women and are probably also overclassifying a minority of men with risks and needs more similar to those of female offenders than to those of their fellow male offenders.

Burke and Adams offer two recommendations that any well-managed jurisdiction should effect: (1) methodological issues having to do with the smallness of numbers and proportion of women must be resolved within each jurisdiction for risk-based classification to be valid (or legal) for placing women and (2) statewide systems must find ways to accommodate not only women, but also men who are low-risk, but high-need:

It seems, then, that the general thrust of improvement in women's classification is not in the development of better, more specifically women-oriented risk classification tools, but in an approach to classification that supports an emphasis on rehabilitation (Burke & Adams 1991).

Solutions

In reviewing the literature on female offenders—especially in regard to their classification and treatment in state jurisdictions—one is forced to revisit the same profiles and the same problems, again and again.

It is clear from the literature cited throughout this chapter that were enough sound community-based programs genuinely available and open to women, institutional female populations of many state jurisdictions might be reduced. Even if the current rage for punishment (even retribution) were to continue unabated, perhaps prison systems could more cost-effectively house and feed female offenders than they do currently. However, reduction in costs from less secure facilities designs, which are usually cheaper, would not necessarily be saved or avoided because they would need to be diverted to "habilitative" programming that might—if it were focused on substantive programming in education, substance abuse, employment, and parenting—eventually reduce female recidivism.

It is for these reasons that this article has not rehashed the old clinical versus risk classification arguments and applied them to women. It is not that substantive, technical, methodological, and practical issues do not apply; it is that the core issues continue to be unresolved. If—as caseloads suggest—despite litigation, prison administrators continue to have fairly wide discretion in developing and implementing classification systems for their own jurisdictions, why do female offenders still appear to suffer in regard to due process rights and gender equity?

Cost cannot be the reason because a reality-based look at women is likely to lower societal costs, both human and dollar. Also, there is no lack of competent and expert professionals—as is evident by merely reviewing this chapter's reference section. If it is neither cost nor expertise, is it possible that the seventeenth century distinction between worthy and unworthy and the eighteenth and nineteenth century distinction between able-bodied and not able-bodied are alive and well and enshrined in modern day sexism?

> Economic reasons for the disadvantaged position of female prisoners is only part of the story. Even more important is the long-standing influence of sexism, which has come to shape the structure of women's prisons and their programs (Hawkins & Alpert 1989).

Where Next?

Evaluations of existing systems to which some thought and resources have been given, such as in Illinois, South Carolina, and Wyoming, might well be a place for corrections to begin to assess, design, research, and promulgate models for testing whether female offenders and their communities can be served well at this stage of classification art and science. As with other issues, existing and potential biases need to be explored for validity and invalidity, criteria need to be truly objective, and consensus, whether of citizens, staff, or inmates, needs to be investigated for the possibility that agreement on criteria for placing and treating women may—without empirical testing—simply provide future history more cases of correctional "emperors with no clothes."

Avenues that stretch beyond consistency and consensus may already exist. Wyoming's classification system is an example of this (Burke & Adams 1991):

> Classification at the WCC is based on demonstrated behavior and individual progress. In this way, it is in stark contrast to much classification practice in the nation which seeks to anticipate or predict behavior based upon either clinical judgment or empirically derived risk assessment instruments.... [T]he physical environment...controls movement and assures close staff observation. Once within that environment, risk is managed gradually, granting greater levels of movement and independence with a carefully constructed set of incentives to encourage acceptable behavior.... [T]here may be lessons here for larger jurisdictions as well.

In jurisdictions with several institutional and/or community locations appropriate for women, initial assignment might be made via an empirically validated risk assessment similar to that of male inmates in that specific jurisdiction; however, classification and/or "internal" placement be made via a Wyoming-type system. This dual thrust, if monitored and evaluated adequately, could resolve issues of equity/parity and "least restrictive" cost-effectiveness.

References

American Correctional Association. 1993. *Female offenders: Meeting needs of a neglected population.* Laurel, Md.: ACA.

American Correctional Association. 1990. *The female offender: What does the future hold?* Laurel, Md.: ACA.

Brown, Aaron A., Charlotte A. Nesbitt, and Angela R. Argento. 1984. *Female classification: An examination of the issues.* Washington, D.C.: National Institute of Corrections.

Burke, Peggy, and Linda Adams. 1991. *Classification of women offenders in state correctional facilities: A handbook for practitioners.* Washington, D.C.: National Institute of Corrections.

Hawkins, Richard, and Geoffrey P. Alpert. 1987. *American prison systems: Punishment and justice.* New York: Prentice Hall.

Pierce, Glenn, et al. 1991. *The classification of male and female offenders by the Massachusetts probation system.* Boston: Center for Applied Social Research, Northeastern University.

V. Risk Assessment: An Evaluation of Statistical Classification Methods

By Tim Brennan, Ph.D.

An unfortunate gap exists between the statistical technologies available for risk assessment and their actual incorporation into corrections. To date, only the most basic statistical risk assessment methods have been generally incorporated into applied corrections. In part, the slow dissemination and implementation of more advanced techniques has resulted from a practical need for efficiency, ease of use, high-face validity, and ease of training in the crowded world of corrections. These represent barriers for any method that is computationally intensive or sophisticated. Yet, new computer software with greater computation power is rapidly diminishing these barriers.

Other reasons for failure must be laid squarely on the poor design and inadequate validation of many of the statistical methods that have achieved some foothold in corrections (Kane 1986; Wright et al. 1984; Clear 1988; MacKenzie 1988; Brennan 1987). Methods that have been introduced are often based on primitive statistical assumptions, unreliable or irrelevant data, and violations of virtually every tenet of measurement theory. Design flaws abounded in many of the risk assessment schemes introduced. Nevertheless, several of these methods were adopted by correctional facilities without sufficient cross-validation to assess whether they work or not in local jurisdictions (Alexander & Austin 1992).

However, there are guarded reasons for optimism. Many jails, prisons, and other correctional agencies are adopting statistical risk assessment procedures, and there seems to be a heightened awareness that validation and predictive efficiency should not be taken for granted.

Tim Brennan, Ph.D., is research director of Northpoint Institute for Public Management and an associate professor at Colorado University.

Prediction and risk assessment remain ubiquitous in correctional decision making (e.g., release on recognizance, granting of probation and parole, levels of custody within correctional facilities, house arrest, community placements at various levels of supervision). There is virtually no type of decision that is not influenced by risk assessments (Glaser 1987).

Many correctional decision makers face increasing financial and legal pressure to avoid false positive errors, avoid waste, achieve least restrictive custody, and aid the correctional decision maker in reaching valid and justifiable decisions. Statistical risk assessment seems destined to assume a larger role in correctional decision making.

Risk assessment is implicit in many fundamental correctional policies (Brennan 1987b; MacKenzie 1988; Alexander 1986). For example, the concept of least restrictive custody depends on, and requires, a valid risk assessment. This policy, in fact, cannot be implemented in the absence of an assessment of degree of risk. The bottom line is that even in their present state of development, statistical risk assessment methods offer sufficient predictive validity when properly used.

Preliminary Concepts: Base Rates, Selection Ratio, and Cross-validation

Human versus Statistical Risk Assessment

A critical question for risk assessment instruments is: how successful are they in predicting individual offenders' outcome behaviors? Many studies, across numerous outcome behaviors (i.e., recidivism, suicides, violent crimes, etc.), show that present predictive methods, although offering significant improvements over chance, have only modest predictive validity (Gottfredson 1987; Farrington 1987; Alexander & Austin 1992). The explained (predicted) variance for many risk instruments is only about 15 percent to 20 percent of offender outcome behaviors (Gottfredson & Gottfredson 1986; Craddock 1988). Yet, while such predictions only modestly exceed chance, some have suggested that if these risk assessment systems were implemented, they would improve criminal justice decision making (Gottfredson 1987). This raises the issue of how statistical risk procedures compare to human decision making.

In comparing statistical versus practitioner/expert judgment across various fields (medicine, corrections, biology, psychiatry, and so on) it is almost universally found that statistical prediction outperforms human judgments in virtually every systematic comparison study (Meehl 1954; Gottfredson 1987). Even where the statistical device uses a smaller set of data than is available to the human judge, it can produce superior accuracy (Meehl 1954). For example, in studies of parole decisions, it has been shown that statistical methods outperformed judgments of psychiatrists and sociologists (Glaser 1955, 1962; Gottfredson & Beverly 1962). Carroll et al. (1982) found that parole board members' judgments were virtually uncorrelated with behavioral outcomes, while a statistical model modestly outperformed the board. In predicting recidivism, Holland et al. (1983) found that a statistical risk assessment outperformed both mental health professionals and correctional case workers.

A prevailing skepticism about statistical procedures, however, is still warranted because they have only moderate predictive validity and will make a fair number of false positive and false negative errors. Thus, the reluctance to "go by the numbers" is likely to persist in correctional decision making. The weaknesses of current (and past) risk assessment devices have laid them open to attack—for example, narrowness of the data, flawed statistical methods (many past risk assessment devices had minimal statistical bases), and the inability to account for "mitigating circumstances." Yet, most predictive instruments are developed using large databases filled with redundant, irrelevant, and correlated factors (Glaser 1987). The statistical process then narrows this down to the most optimally predictive risk factors. The initial database for these statistical procedures is thus as broad, or broader, than that used by the subjective human decision maker.

Subjective risk assessment has also had substantial criticism for high error rates. Use of spurious risk factors, ignoring base rates, erroneous weighting of nonpredictive factors, and ineffective heuristics are widespread in human decision making in corrections and unfortunately become more frequent under crowded and pressured conditions (Brennan 1985).

False Positives and False Negatives

When appropriate outcome data are collected, risk assessment predictions can be compared with actual outcomes using a simple cross-classification table. The simplest table occurs when risk (both predicted and outcome) is dichotomized into low or high and these predictions are cross-classified with behavioral outcomes in a basic 2×2 table (see Figure 1). Figure 1 indicates "correct hits" and two categories of prediction error.

Figure 1
A Cross-classification of Actual Versus Predicted Outcomes in a
2×2 Contingency Table

ACTUAL OUTCOME BEHAVIOR

	High Risk	Low Risk
High Risk	**True positive** (positive hit)	**False positive** (Overclassification error)
Low Risk	**False negative** (underclassification error)	**True negative** (negative hit)

PREDICTED BEHAVIOR

The information presented in such a contingency table allows an assessment of the predictive accuracy of various risk assessment methods. A general categorization of these four cells is as follows:

49

1. False positives are predicted to be high-risk but exhibit no problem behavior.

2. False negatives are predicted to be low-risk, but eventually commit the high-risk behavior.

3. True negatives are predicted as low-risk and show no problem behavior.

4. True positives are predicted as high-risk and will exhibit the predicted negative behavior.

When risk predictions are based on a linear additive scale (the most common method in corrections) some cutting points are imposed on the distribution of risk scores to separate low risks from high risks. Changing the location of the "cutting points" will profoundly change the rates for both kinds of prediction errors. For example, if practitioners are concerned about false negative errors, they can minimize these by changing the cutting point on a risk scale so that very high percentages of offenders are predicted as high-risks. This reduces the number of cases assigned to low-risk cells, and thus reduces the number of false negatives. To avoid false negatives, correctional agencies often shift cutting points toward the restrictive end of the scale. This minimizes the occurrences of false negatives at the cost of erroneously labelling many offenders as high-risk, and producing more false positive errors. This tendency often occurs because correctional staff are often judged only when something goes wrong— such errors are highly visible and staff are held accountable. The relative "visibility" of these two errors differs. The false negative error, which by definition produces a visible "incident," inexorably becomes the primary criterion on which staff are judged and supervised.

The Base Rate for Criterion Behavior

The base rate for criterion behavior refers to the actual rate of occurrence of the outcome (e.g., parole revocation, violent recidivism, escape, suicides, and so on). Each of these outcomes will occur at a certain percentage or rate. A base rate is the frequency with which a criterion behavior or outcome occurs in a particular population over a specified period of time. It is usually expressed as a percentage or proportion for the time period being considered (Gottfredson 1987). The base rate is the marginal distribution in Figure 1 for the "actual" high-risk behavior. Base rates for criterion behavior, such as suicide, violence, and escape, are all very low—ranging from 3 percent to less than 1 percent (Chapman & Alexander 1981). The base rate is critical because it governs the predictive efficiency of any risk assessment device. As a base rate deviates from 50 percent, and comes closer to 0, predictive efficiency is more difficult to achieve.

Base Rates and Predictive Efficiency

Predictive efficiency is the extent to which a predictive device produces an improvement over the prediction offered by the base rate for a particular group. When a base rate for an outcome behavior is, say 65 percent, a 65 percent accuracy rate can be obtained simply by classifying all offenders as high risks. Thus, the predictive device must reach an accuracy of 65 percent or higher before it offers any predictive advantage. Conversely, if the base rate for violent recidivism is 3 percent, 97 percent correct classification is automatically obtained by assigning all offenders to the low-risk category. Thus, the base rate becomes the figure to beat for prediction devices. When an extreme base rate exists (e.g., 90 percent) a predictive device must reach a predictive accuracy of at least 90 percent to offer a useful advantage over the base rate. The closer the base rate is to 50 percent, the better chance a predictive device has of providing a meaningful improvement in predictive accuracy. Yet, this is often not the case in corrections.

A statistical risk assessment device begins to have clear advantage when it creates subcategories in which "within-category" base rates are much different from that of the overall sample and substantially different from 50 percent. Prediction becomes progressively more difficult, and errors more frequent, as the base rate deviates from 50 percent (Meehl & Rosen 1955). Very frequent, or very infrequent, events will be predicted with more errors. Rare events incur more false positive errors, while common events incur more false negatives.

Glaser (1987) notes that much of the failure of predictive devices in corrections stems from their use in situations where criterion base rates are relatively rare (close to 0 percent, e.g., suicide, escape, etc). Glaser notes that parole boards, psychiatrists, and others frequently make predictions regarding outcome behaviors that are rare (e.g., less than 10 percent) and make such decisions with confidence and certainty. These are safe decisions because when an offender is assigned a high-risk label, it becomes impossible to check the validity of these predictions.

The Selection Ratio of an Assessment Device

The selection ratio is commonly understood as the percentage of cases classified by the prediction device into the outcome or criterion behavior. For example, the percentage of offenders classified in the habitual criminal category by a scale for habitual criminals is the selection ratio for that scale. The selection ratio is the marginal frequencies in a 2×2 contingency table for the predicted outcome.

Different risk assessment procedures may have different selection ratios. For example, restrictive instruments assign more offenders to a high-risk category, while liberal instruments make fewer such assignments. The cutting scores on a predictive scale directly determine the selection ratio, as well as the marginal distributions for the high- and low-risk rows. Any changes in cutting points will also change the selection ratio and the kind of errors made by a risk assessment scale.

Construction Samples and Validation Samples

In developing risk assessment instruments, a sample of offenders that is representative of a specific population, risk decision, and time period is typically used. This is often called a construction sample. It must be large enough for statistical stability and representative enough to generalize to the population of concern. Furthermore, a follow-up period must provide sufficient time to allow the outcome behaviors to occur. Thus, recidivism studies must have a sufficiently long follow-up period to avoid underestimating the occurrence of recidivism.

Many statistical procedures used to develop risk prediction scales (e.g., multiple regression, discriminant analysis, predictive attribute analysis) are optimization devices in that they will always optimize predictive accuracy for the construction sample. Thus, they often produce an "overfit" between the new risk assessment device and the particular data structures of the construction sample. When the device is then used on another sample, predictive accuracy usually shrinks. The predictive accuracy of a new device is usually inflated when assessed on a construction sample. A cross-validation sample is required to obtain an unbiased estimate of expected predictive efficiency (Tabacknick & Fidell 1989).

Dimensional versus Categorical/Configural Methods

The most common kind of correctional risk assessment has been the additive point scale, which is one type of dimensional scaling in which several risk factors are combined into a single score. There are many approaches to constructing scales (e.g., psychometric scaling, factor analysis, regression analysis, discriminant analysis). The end point of all scaling is a single "scaled value" for each offender. The object of combining diverse risk factors is to eliminate the effect of "error variance" and random fluctuations, to avoid the special perspective of each separate indicator, and to produce a set of numbers that best reflects the variability among offenders (Jacoby 1991). Thus, a scaling process combines several incomplete or partial pieces of information into an estimate of a single geometric or dimensional model.

The geometric model is a straight line, with offenders scoring from low to high on this dimension (Jacoby 1991). In many applications of risk assessment, a common practice is to impose boundaries or cutting points on the additive scale to form categories. This is used in jail and prison custody classifications where (usually) two cutting points are applied to break a scale distribution into three categories (maximum, medium, and minimum). Since the work of Burgess (1928), a stream of additive point scales have been developed, such as those used in the Wisconsin probation and parole system (Baird et al. 1979); VERA-type pretrial risk assessments, such as those used in the California inmate classification system (Holt et al. 1981); and multifactor scales for custody classifications (Bonta & Motiuk 1992).

Categorical, taxonomic, or configural methods in contrast create category systems where each offender is placed into a qualitatively different category. This approach does not use a single score, but places an offender into a group that is categorized by a profile or configuration of scores. For example, a configural score in a decision tree might define an inmate as appropriate for maximum security when there is a pattern of current violent offense, prior violent convictions, and prior disciplinary/behavioral problems. This configuration defines the meaning of the category, and all offenders who have these three characteristics are assigned to the maximum security class. This approach organizes and uses information in a different format than dimensional scaling.

Statistical Methods for Risk Assessment: A Selected Review

This section provides brief reviews of several statistical approaches to constructing both dimensional and configural risk assessments. (Detailed reviews are provided by Gottfredson [1987], Fildes and Gottfredson [1968], Brennan [1987a, 1987b], and Glaser [1987]). Different methods are preferred by different users for various methodological, theoretical, and interpretative reasons. The choice of a method clearly depends on assumptions about the form of the data, the different output or information needed by users, and the appropriateness of different mathematical and statistical models for the purposes of the user.

The Unweighted Additive Points Approach

The simplest approach is the unweighted additive points approach of Burgess (1928). This method involves the selection of several risk factors, each weighted as 0 (if absent) and 1 (if present). There is no differential weighting to take predictive saliency into account. The total score is calculated and used for predictive purposes.

The procedure, and variants of it, have received widespread use for risk assessment in corrections. Several recent studies have found that the method compares quite favorably to more sophisticated systems (Gottfredson & Gottfredson 1979).

However, the method has several disadvantages. It has virtually no statistical justification, does not account for correlations and redundancies among different risk factors, and gives no indication of the relative predictive power of the different factors because they are all assumed to be equal. Thus, aside from users not knowing which variables are redundant, they cannot know which factors are irrelevant, and so they do not have the needed information to fine-tune or improve the procedure (e.g., by dropping irrelevant and redundant items, adding new items with higher predictive value).

Weighted Additive Point Scales

A variant of the Burgess procedure is the differential weighting of predictive risk factors according to perceived relative importance. Weighting factors can be developed by statistical procedures (e.g., multiple regression, discriminant analysis, etc.) or can be imposed subjectively through the consensus of users. A recent example of differential weighting is the development of a jail custody screening form supported by the National Institute of Corrections (Austin 1991; Austin et al. 1990). This national project produced a screening classification system using a weighted approach for the following risk factors:

- severity of current charges/convictions
- seriousness of offense history
- escape history
- institutional discipline history
- prior felony convictions
- alcohol/drug use
- social stability factors (age, employment, residence)

In many such systems, the selection and weighting of the factors is not guided by a statistical procedure but is reached by the consensus judgment of corrections officials and expert practitioners. This was the procedure followed in designing custody screening systems for jails (Austin et al. 1990).

In the consensus approach to risk factor selection, the current practices of inmate custody classification as used in correctional facilities serves as a starting point. The rationale is to build on the expert knowledge of experienced practitioners. A major focus of the NCCD/CSG survey (Austin et al. 1990) was to identify elements that were common to jail classification approaches across the country. As might be expected, there were many different methods of custody screening in the many additive scales used in jails nationally. Sixty jails provided information on their classification procedures and policies, and these prior methods served as a starting point for the NCCD/CSG scale development project.

Such practitioner selections represent implicit theories, or hypotheses, regarding institutional custody risks (DeVellis 1991). In the absence of statistical validation, they can be seen only as conventional wisdom or guesswork. The validity of each item must be confirmed or disconfirmed through appropriate validation studies (Kane 1986; Wright et al. 1984).

Recently, much criticism has been leveled at the nonstatistical basis and poor psychometric properties of such additive scaling procedures in corrections (Wright et al. 1984; Glaser 1987) and at the inadequacy of information given to officers who use such systems (MacKenzie 1988). A single scale score is not seen as providing sufficiently detailed information for the full range of decisions that must be made by line officers. Low predictive validity has also become an issue. For both statistically and consensus-generated procedure, it is critical that they be revalidated and checked for predictive validity in any new correctional setting where they will be used (Wright et al. 1984; Alexander & Austin 1992). The predictive validity of screening procedures developed at one time and place do not always transfer to other jurisdictions.

Multiple Regression Models

Multiple regression has been the most frequently used procedure for developing risk assessment devices. It is used widely not only in corrections, but in most applied social sciences for prediction and risk assessment (Tabachnick & Fidell 1989). Of the many variants of regression, ordinary least squares (OLS) regression has become the standard model of regression as opposed to other forms (e.g., stepwise regression). The OLS method produces a weighted linear combination of the predictor variables that mathematically minimize errors in computing predicted scores.

Multiple regression is based on a well-developed statistical theory that can indicate the relative importance of the different risk predictors, assess error levels in making predictions, and give significance tests (using t-tests or F-ratios) of the predictive validity of each risk factor. The relative validity of different risk factors is indicated when they are standardized to a common metric (usually Z scores).

Knowledge of the relative predictive validity of different risk factors is useful for progressively refining new instruments. It allows irrelevant factors to be dropped and new hypothesized risk factors to be evaluated. This produces time and cost savings. Multiple regression also helps with the problem of correlated risk factors and minimizes any redundancy or double counting of correlated variables. Once the information content (or predictive power) of a particular variable has been introduced into the stepwise regression, other correlated variables receive little weight.

This flexible technique can be extended to include both nonlinear effects and complex interactions between risk factors, for example, the joint predictive effect of several factors. Nonlinear terms are introduced into the regression by using polynomials. Interaction effects between predictors are introduced as multiplicative terms. Predicted outcome scores are easily computed using the regression equation in its unstandardized form, with unstandardized regression weights applied to the raw risk factor scores. The method has proved useful in numerous studies and has been found to outperform human judgment in predictive accuracy in virtually every area where it has been tested (Meehl 1954; Glaser 1987).

However, multiple regression is not a panacea and has several problems that may be serious in some situations:

1. There are situations where data relations (either predictive factors or outcomes) are not linear, which violates a basic assumption of linear regression.

2. Although multiple regression can handle complex interaction effects, the procedures are cumbersome, difficult to interpret, and usually excluded in most applications.

3. When multicollinearity exists (i.e., where predictor variables themselves are highly correlated) the regression model may become uninterpretable and unstable (Tabachnick & Fidell 1989).

4. Multimodalities or type-effects may occur in corrections data.

5. Many correctional variables are not measured as interval scales and do not have normal distributions. Many are dichotomous (e.g., parole violator or not) or categorical.

6. Multiple regression, as well as other more sophisticated methods, has not been found to produce much greater predictive accuracy than simpler methods in several comparative studies (Gottfredson & Gottfredson 1979).

Two-dimensional Matrix Classifications

A popular variant of the additive scaling approach is to cross-classify two separate categorical scales and provide a simple cross-classification matrix or a grid with several cells. Each cell represents a different risk profile and different policies may be designed for each category.

Discriminant Function Analysis

Discriminant function techniques can also be used to develop risk assessment devices when the outcome is a set of categories in contrast to

57

multiple regression, which is used to predict continuous outcomes. Discriminant function analysis has had little use in applied corrections. This method cannot create new categories (as does cluster analysis or configural methods), but must begin with a development sample in which groups are already categorized into criterion levels (e.g., suicides, attempted suicides, and nonattempters). The method identifies the predictive risk factors with the most significant discriminating power between criterion classes and produces optimally weighted additive scales.

Because the predictive power of each risk factor is indicated by its weight on the discriminant function, the method identifies factors with high and low validity. This helps in designing new scales and in eliminating irrelevant factors. The stepwise variant of the discriminant function—operating in the same manner as stepwise regression—can be used to discover predictively optimal subsets of risk factors and to eliminate redundant and irrelevant factors. A useful output from discriminant analysis is a "hit-rate" table that gives detailed information on the predictive success in classifying subjects into their correct criterion classes. It indicates the percentage of cases correctly classified and the false negative and positive errors.

Another useful calculation is the probability of membership of each offender to each predicted outcome group. Thus, an offender may have a probability of 0.85 of being a member of group A and low probabilities of membership in groups B, C, and D. Such probabilities can identify offenders who are unambiguously classified into one group or, conversely, those who are "hybrids" and ambiguously classified (e.g., similar probabilities of belonging to several groups).

Like multiple regression, the discriminant function procedure capitalizes on unique features of the construction sample and will inflate predictive accuracy.

Multidimensional Contingency Table Analysis

Log linear models are well-suited to risk assessment and the data used in corrections, particularly when predictive factors are measured at categorical or nominal levels (Gottfredson 1987). The method offers an advanced way of analyzing contingency table data when using categorical predictors and where, at most, relations of ordering are obtained between categories. Thus, it deals with data types where multiple regression and other linear models provide a modest or poor fit. It does not require the assumption of multivariate normal distributions to conduct significance tests and makes fewer assumptions about the nature of the variables or relations between them.

A disadvantage of the method is the need for large samples, particularly when many risk factors are being studied simultaneously, which is often the case in corrections.

Clustering Analysis

In the past fifteen years corrections has added taxometric clustering methods to its arsenal for constructing classifications and risk assessment schemes. The well-known offender typology of Megargee and Bohn (1980) was constructed with Ward's clustering method. Many correctional facilities have adopted this system. The past decade has seen a steady production of new offender classification systems developed with various clustering methods and used for predictive, treatment, and management purposes.

In evaluating the use of cluster analysis for risk assessment an important point is that there is no single "best" method for all purposes. Different data, goals, and problems will require different classification strategies. Thus, the problem is to select a method that best fits the data and purpose.

Hierarchical Agglomerative Clustering

Agglomerative clustering methods embody the same series of steps:

1. Assess all offenders on a common set of risk factors.

2. Compute a similarity metric for each offender and all other offenders to produce a similarity matrix among offenders.

3. Start clustering by joining the most similar pair of offenders into a new cluster.

4. Join the next closest pair; this may include joining a single offender to a previously created cluster.

5. Continue this joining (agglomeration) until all offenders are grouped together in a single large cluster.

6. Choose a level of the hierarchical agglomeration process as a basis to study the resulting homogenous groups of offenders.

This agglomerative process sequentially joins offenders together into homogeneous groups to produce a hierarchical tree called a "dendrogram." This illustrates all fusions at successive similarity levels.

Several well-known statistical programs offer important forms of agglomerative clustering. An example in corrections is Henderson's (1982) work with incarcerated homicides. Using two methods of clustering, Henderson replicated and extended the typology of homicides offered by Blackburn (1970, 1974). She found several replicable classes: (1) disturbed psychotic hostile, with high family violence, (2) extraverted undercontrolled and hostile, (3) inhibited, introverted, overcontrolled, few friends, and (4) controlled and nonpsychotic. Officers in most jails can readily identify these on a subjective basis and are well-aware of the quiet, well-behaved inmate serving time for homicide.

K-means Partitioning

K-means partitioning is an alternative to agglomerative clustering when analyzing large data sets. An advantage is that the "trial placement" of an offender into a class can be corrected if the early assignment is in error because the method can correct its own mistakes. The basic steps include the following:

1. A set of trial cluster centers is chosen.
2. Each offender is compared to these "initial" centers and assigned to the closest (most similar) center.
3. The centroids of these classes are recalculated and used as new cluster centers.
4. Similarities of all offenders to the new cluster centers are recomputed, and they are reassigned to the nearest center.
5. This process iterates until it converges on a stable classification where there is no further improvement in an algebraic function of the quality of the classification and no reassignments can be made.

Assessing the Accuracy of Predictive Devices

The basic aim of risk assessment is accurate prediction, a minimum of errors, and an improvement in prediction over the base rate. In considering the advantages of various risk assessment approaches, users have measured predictive efficiency in many different ways. It is critical that any evaluations of predictive efficiency should be made only when the device is tested on a cross-validation sample because, if predictive validity assessment is based on the basis of a construction sample, it will always be inflated (Tabacknick & Fidell 1989).

The Overall Hit Rate

The simplest approach uses the earlier 2 x 2 contingency table and is a tally of overall "correct hits"—where predictions matched outcomes. This is given by adding the total correct hits and dividing by the number of offenders in the sample. Unfortunately, this intuitively simple approach does not show how much improvement the device achieves over the base rate nor what would be expected by random assignment into the cells. However, it is a useful starting point and offers an informal evaluation of the predictive efficiency of a device.

Chi-square and Correlational Indices

The basic cross-classification table between predicted versus actual outcomes (e.g., Figure 1) also provides the data to measure the statistical association between predicted and actual scores. Most statistical packages provide several measures of the overall strength of this relationship (e.g., chi-square, contingency coefficient, Cramer's V, Goodman and Kruskal's lambda). These give a good idea of the strength of association and the statistical significance of this relationship. The Phi coefficient, for example, is formally identical to the well-known Pearson's correlation coefficient (r), and in the 2×2 contingency table offers a general measure of predictive accuracy (Gottfredson 1987). Yet, these general association measures are also influenced by variations in the base rate and do not allow consistent comparisons of predictive methods across different base rate levels. They are useful in comparing the relative performance of predictive devices within specific offender populations and for specific decisions (Gottfredson 1987; Brennan et al. 1980).

Proportional Reduction in Error Indices

Several methods have been developed to estimate reduction in error compared to that which would be given strictly using the base rate for prediction. Using the base rate as the bottom line for statistical accuracy, these indices indicate the percent reduction in error that would be made when using the predictive device. For example, if a 30 percent error rate can be expected when using base rate considerations (say in the prediction of violent recidivism) and a 15 percent error rate is achieved with the predictive instrument, then errors have been reduced by approximately 50 percent. Thus, these indices are known as "proportional reduction in error" indices.

Ohlin and Duncan's (1949) index of predictive efficiency compares errors obtained using any predictive instrument with errors obtained using the base rate alone. This index is also sensitive to base rate, and any conclusions may not generalize across situations that have different base rates (Gottfredson 1987).

Relative Improvement over Chance

Indices that estimate the improvement given by a predictive device compared to chance are becoming more prevalent in corrections in assessing predictive efficiency (Loeber & Dishion 1983; Bonta & Motiuk 1992). This kind of index was introduced to avoid the dependency on the base rate.

This approach weakens dependency on both the selection ratio and base rate. This index is not totally independent of either the base rate or the selection ratio but less dependent on these than the index of predictive efficiency (Farrington 1987).

Mean Cost Rating

This index incorporates a comparison of the benefits of the risk classification (e.g., the correct matches) and the relative cost of errors. A basic assumption is that any predictive device must be evaluated according to utilities and costs (Duncan et al. 1953; Duncan & Duncan 1955; Glaser 1987). This index gives a measure of the general predictive power of the device without constraints placed by the base rates and selection ratios. Thus, it can be used to make more general assessments of predictive efficiency irrespective of base rate conditions. The index ranges from zero when the base rates of all the categories are identical (a classification system offers minimal predictive accuracy above the base rate of all base rate levels of risk categories are identical) to a high of 1.0 when there is perfect separation of the criterion behaviors between the classes.

Conclusions

Improved Data Collection and Verification

Corrections needs to upgrade measurement levels, reliability, and completeness of the data used in risk assessment. No prediction instrument can be better than the data on which it was constructed and which drives its use. One of the reasons given for the failure of newer statistical models to improve over simple, unweighted additive scaling was that correctional data on which the methods were tested were poor (Gottfredson & Gottfredson 1979). Thus, better statistical models on their own may not produce any advantage until correctional data are improved.

Much of the data collected in corrections are worthless, haphazardly recorded, filled with unverified opinion, and derived from official case files that are notorious for missing and unreliable data (Glaser 1987; Gottfredson 1987; Austin 1983). Farrington (1987) notes that official outcomes data (e.g., disciplinary infractions, recidivism) also are of poor quality. Goldkamp (1987) noted that despite poor validity, unreliability, and measurement weakness in official criminal histories, these are frequently used in predictive devices. It is ironic that computerized information systems—in the absence of any improvement of data collection and measurement—may result in unreliable data now being more highly accessible for analysis and (faulty) decision making.

Improved Psychometric Measurement

Another feature that has plagued corrections is its blind spot regarding measurement and psychometric qualities of risk assessment scales. There have been many calls to establish the validity and reliability of risk assessment scales in corrections, but these have too often been ignored (Solomon 1980; Solomon & Baird 1983). Scale development activity in corrections has historically demonstrated little concern with psychometric properties, statistical validation, or theoretical foundations of the instruments. Few inmate risk classification instruments are developed with careful consideration to validation or measurement qualities (Wright et al. 1984).

An extremely casual approach to statistical validation and measurement theory continues to damage corrections, where many risk assessment instruments of unknown or poor scientific quality go in and out of fashion. There is a continuing need in corrections for better measurement standards, validation of instruments, and defensible psychometric properties (Cheyet et al. 1989; Kane 1986, Clear 1988).

Developing a good rating scale is seldom easy, and informal casual methods of scale construction have numerous pitfalls that can doom the scientific quality and practical usefulness of a scale (Lewis-Beck 1992). Informal approaches are often characterized by poor psychometric and measurement properties (e.g., low reliability, unknown validity, and an awkward ambiguity regarding what the scale actually measures). Low measurement reliability can blur differences between offenders, false positive and false negative errors proliferate, predictive power is minimal, and any confidence in the validity of the instrument is lost. The costs of poorly constructed scales generally outweigh their benefits (DeVellis 1991).

Yet, many newly developed custody and security scales and pretrial release risk scales developed in the past decade were introduced into facility operations without fundamental measurement procedures, such as item-analysis and scale reliability assessment, without knowledge of basic reliability coefficients, such as Cronbach's alpha, and without validation. Fortunately, there are signs that the problem of measurement quality is being taken more seriously (Clear 1988; Kane 1986; Alexander & Austin 1992).

Multimodal data sources and multiple criteria offer useful ways to improve measurement quality. Predictions may be improved if data from several sources were combined because this may overcome errors and biases inherent in any single source (Farrington 1987). Many correctional variables can be measured by self-reports, official records, and different observers. The value of self-report data has been demonstrated repeatedly. Chaiken and Chaiken (1982) found that predictions based on self-report data were, in fact, more accurate than predictions based on official records. Multiple criteria from several sources are available in corrections yet are seldom combined to produce more valid and reliable indicators.

Improved Content Validity

Another weakness of risk assessment in corrections is inadequate content validity (e.g., the inadequate coverage of salient variables). Problems include the omission of critical variables, the inclusion of irrelevant variables, redundancy, and an absence of theoretical coherence.

Sechrest (1987) complains that variable selection in most prior-offender assessment systems suffer from narrowness, oversimplification, and lack of theoretical guidance. The tendency to throw together some risk factors without much theoretical guidance is a major culprit in poor content validity. Glaser (1987) noted that most existing risk assessment instruments are dominated by an atheoretical search for predictive factors, guesswork, and conventional wisdom. Farrington (1987) states that variable selection has proceeded with blind empiricism, without theoretical guidance, and is often determined primarily or exclusively by what is available in official records. An alternative is that risk variables should be selected in advance based on carefully argued theoretical grounds rather than selected haphazardly. Even where there is no available theory (e.g., jail custody risk assessment) investigators must lay out their own conceptual formulations prior to trying to operationalize them and must specify at least some tentative theoretical model to guide scale development (DeVellis 1991).

Vigilant Local Demonstration of Predictive Validity and Cross-validation

A continuing scandal in corrections is the frequent avoidance of local statistical validation (Wright et al. 1984; Alexander & Austin 1992). Correctional agencies often simply borrow a risk assessment system and modify and use it without conducting any local validation or testing its general application to local offender population. Another common practice is to simply invent a risk assessment system with no validation research.

Improved Statistical Methods

Advanced statistical and quantitative procedures have had minimal use in applied corrections. Any method that requires line officers to do much more than simple arithmetic is perceived as being too mathematically cumbersome, too inefficient, or too advanced for successful introduction into applied corrections. As a result, simple decision trees, which involve no arithmetic and additive point scales, are generally the most advanced techniques used in applied corrections. Multiple regression methods are sometimes used, and more sophisticated methods are rare.

Constraints on advanced techniques have resulted partly from the need for exceptionally user-friendly methods, lack of training among corrections staff in statistical risk assessment or measurement techniques, and inadequate computerization. Staff are generally overworked and under severe psychological and organizational pressure to avoid any false-negative errors. Thus, a highly conservative and streamlined decision style has tended to dominate (Brennan 1985; MacKenzie 1988).

The advent of flexible management information systems software for storage, retrieval, data analysis, and automation of mathematical functions will profoundly change this situation. For example, risk assessment scales developed with discriminant functions or log-linear models can be programmed and embedded into facility database software. The staff will be shielded from complex arithmetic and the statistical "expertise" will be embedded in new correctional software and rendered user friendly. Local validation of complex statistical models on the correctional organization's own population data will remain critical. Thus, a reasonable expectation is that more advanced statistical and data analysis techniques will be gradually incorporated into correctional software for risk assessment and decision making. This should produce a quantum leap in predictive accuracy—but only if data collection and content validity issues are also upgraded. From a political perspective, it is critical that such statistically driven risk assessment procedures be viewed as advisory and not as making a final decision. The human judge must always have an override capacity to introduce the intuitive, holistic, integrative role and to take into account any extraneous mitigating issues.

References

Alexander, J. A. 1986. Classification objectives and practices. *Crime and Delinquency* 32:323–38.

Alexander, J. A., and J. Austin. 1992. *Handbook for evaluating objective prison classification systems*. San Francisco: National Council on Crime and Delinquency.

Austin, J. 1983. Assessing the new generation of prison classification models. *Crime and Delinquency* 29:561–76.

Austin, J. 1991. Objective jail classification—screening jail inmates: An effective tool for improving security. *Corrections Today* 53 (July): 80–85.

Baird, C. 1979. *The Wisconsin case classification/staff management project: A two-year follow-up*. Madison, Wisc.: Wisconsin Bureau of Community Corrections.

Blackburn, R. 1971. Personality types among abnormal homicides. *British Journal of Criminology* 11:14–31.

Blackburn, R. 1975. An empirical classification of psychopathic personality. *British Journal of Psychiatry*. 127:456–60.

Bonta, J., and L. L. Motiuk. 1992. Inmate classification. *Journal of Criminal Justice* 20:343–53.

Brennan, T. 1985. *Offender classification and its relation to jail overcrowding*. Boulder, Colo.: National Institute of Corrections, Information Center.

Brennan, T. 1980. *Multivariate taxonomic classification for criminal justice. Final report*. Washington, D.C.: National Institute of Justice.

Brennan, T. 1987a. Classification: An overview of selected methodological issues. In *Prediction and classification: Criminal justice decision making*, ed. D. M. Gottfredson and M. Tonry. Chicago: University of Chicago Press.

Brennan, T. 1987b. Classification for control in jails and prisons. In *Prediction and classification: Criminal justice decision making*, ed. D. M. Gottfredson and M. Tonry. Chicago: University of Chicago Press.

Burgess, E. W. 1928. Factors determining successes or failures on parole. In *The workings of the indeterminate sentence law and the parole system in Illinois*, ed. A. W. Bruce, E. W. Burgess, and A. J. Harno. Springfield, Ill.: Illinois Board of Parole.

Carroll, J. S., et al. 1982. Evaluation, diagnosis and prediction in parole decision making. *Law and Society Review* 17:199–288.

Chaiken, J. M., and M. R. Chaiken. 1982. *Varieties of criminal behavior*. Santa Monica, Calif.: Rand Corporation.

Chapman, W., and J. Alexander. 1981. *Adjustment to prison: A review of inmate characteristics associated with misconduct, victimization and self-injury in confinement*. Albany, N.Y.: New York State Department of Corrections.

Cheyet, E. F., et al. 1989. *Classification for custody and the assessment of risk in the Colorado Department of Corrections.* New Brunswick, N.J.: Rutgers University School of Criminal Justice.

Clear, T. 1988. Statistical prediction in corrections. *Research in Corrections* 1:1–40.

Craddock, A. 1988. *Inmate classification as organizational social control: Implications for population management.* Chapel Hill, N.C.: University of North Carolina. Doctorate thesis.

DeVellis, R. F. 1991. *Scale development: Theory and applications.* Beverly Hills, Calif.: Sage Publications.

Duncan, O. D., and B. Duncan. 1955. A methodological analysis of segregation indexes. *American Sociological Review* 20:210–17.

Duncan, O. D., et al. 1952. Formal devices for making selection decisions. *American Journal of Sociology* 58:573–84.

Farrington, D. P. 1987. Predicting individual crime rates. In *Prediction and classification: Criminal justice decision making*, ed. D. M. Gottfredson and M. Tonry. Chicago: University of Chicago Press.

Fildes, R., and D. M. Gottfredson. 1969. Cluster analysis in a parolee sample. *Journal of Research in Crime and Delinquency* 5:2–11.

Glaser, D. 1955. The efficacy of alternative approaches to parole prediction. *American Sociological Review* 20:283–87.

Glaser, D. 1962. Prediction tales as accounting devices for judges and parole boards. *Crime and Delinquency* 8:239–58.

Glaser, D. 1987. Classification for risk. In *Prediction and classification: Criminal justice decision making*, ed. D. M. Gottfredson and M. Tonry. Chicago: University of Chicago Press.

Goldkamp, J. S. 1987. Prediction in criminal justice policy development. In *Prediction and classification: Criminal justice decision making*, ed. D. M. Gottfredson and M. Tonry. Chicago: University of Chicago Press.

Gottfredson, D. M., and R. F. Beverly. 1962. Development and operational use of prediction methods in correctional work. In *Proceedings of the social statistics section.* Washington, D.C.: American Statistical Association.

Gottfredson, D. M., and S. D. Gottfredson. 1979. *Screening for risk: A comparison of methods.* Washington, D.C.: National Institute of Corrections.

Gottfredson, D. M., and S. D. Gottfredson. 1986. The accuracy of prediction models. In *Research in criminal careers and career criminals* 2, ed. A. Blumstein et al. Washington, D.C.: National Academy Press.

Gottfredson, S. D. 1987. Prediction: An overview of selected methodological issues. In *Prediction and classification: Criminal justice decision making*, ed. D. M. Gottfredson and M. Tonry. Chicago: University of Chicago Press.

Henderson, M. 1982. An empirical classification of convicted violent offenders. *British Journal of Criminology* 22 (No. 1): 1–21.

Holland, T. R., et al. 1983. Comparison and combination of clinical and statistical predictions of recidivism among adult offenders. *Journal of Applied Psychology* 68:203–11.

Holt, N., G. Ducat, and G. Eakles. 1982. California's new inmate classification system. In *Classification as a management tool: theories and models for decision makers*. College Park, Md.: American Correctional Association.

Jacoby, W. G. 1991. *Data theory and dimensional analysis*. Beverly Hills, Calif.: Sage Publications.

Kane, T. 1986. The validity of prison classification: An introduction to practical considerations and research issues. *Crime and Delinquency* 32 (No. 3): 367–90.

Lewis-Beck, M. S. 1992. *Applied regression: An introduction*. Beverly Hills: Sage Publications.

Loeber, R., and T. Dishion. 1983. Early predictors of male delinquency: A review. *Psychological Bulletin* 94:68–99.

MacKenzie, D. 1988. Prison classification: The management and psychological perspectives. In *The American prison: Issues in research and policy*. Plenum Press.

Meehl, P. E. 1954. *Clinical versus statistical prediction*. Minneapolis: University of Minnesota Press.

Meehl, P. E., and A. Rosen. 1955. Antecedent probability and the efficiency of psychometric signs, patterns or cutting scores. *Psychological Bulletin* 52:194–216.

Megargee, E. I., and M. J. Bohn. 1979. *Classifying criminal offenders: A new approach based on the MMPI*. Beverly Hills, Calif.: Sage Publications.

National Council on Crime and Delinquency/Correctional Services Group.

1990. *Jail classification systems development (executive summary)*. San Francisco: NCCD.

Ohlin, L. E., and O. D. Duncan. 1949. The efficiency of prediction in criminology. *American Journal of Sociology* 54:441–51.

Sechrest, L. 1987. Classification for treatment. In *Prediction and classification: Criminal justice decision making*, ed. D. M. Gottfredson and M. Tonry. Chicago: University of Chicago Press.

Solomon, L. 1980. Developing an empirically based model for classification decision making. *Prison Law Monitor* 217:234–37.

Solomon, L., and C. Baird. 1982. Classification: Past failures and future potential. In *Classification as a management tool: Theories and models for decision makers*. College Park, Md.: American Correctional Association.

Tabachnick, B. G., and L. S. Fidell. 1989. *Using Multivariate Statistics*. New York: Harper and Row.

Wright, K., T. Clear, and P. Dickson. 1984. Universal applicability of probation risk assessment systems: A critique. *Criminology* 22:113–34.

VI. Classification for Internal Management Purposes: The Washington Experience

By James Austin, Ph.D., Christopher Baird, and Deborah Neuenfeldt

P rison classification systems have gained increased attention as prison crowding has reached crisis proportions in many states. Not only have prison populations grown dramatically, but their composition has changed as well. New legislation designed to remove offenders from society for longer periods of time has generally focused on violent, habitual, and more recently, drug offenders.

In Washington, the legislature eliminated indeterminate sentencing and parole, which diverted large numbers of property and first offenders from prison but also increased both the likelihood and length of incarceration for those convicted of violent crimes. As a result, the percentage of violent offenders in Washington's prison population is increasing.

This scenario is being played out at varying degrees in most state prison systems. Although few states have gone as far as Washington has in abolishing indeterminate sentencing, most have passed legislation designed to have similar effects. (Jurisdictions that have abolished parole include Florida, Maine, and the Federal Bureau of Prisons.) Consequently, prison classification and inmate management systems have grown in importance as prison administrators become increasingly concerned about the safety of inmates and staff.

In the late 1970s a new generation of objective classification

This research was supported by Grant #87-IJ-CX-0014 awarded by the National Institute of Justice, U.S. Department of Justice.

James Austin, Ph.D., is an executive vice-president of the National Council on Crime and Delinquency in San Francisco. Christopher Baird is a senior vice-president of NCCD in Madison, Wisconsin. Deborah Neuenfeldt is a research associate with NCCD, Madison.

systems was developed first by the Federal Bureau of Prisons and later by California and the National Institute of Corrections (NIC). Spurred by court orders requiring consistency in correctional decision making and a need to optimally use limited cell space and staff resources, most states now have what are referred to as objective prison classification systems. These systems rely primarily on objective and reliable measures of the inmate's offense severity, prior criminal history, family and social stability, and institutional conduct to designate appropriate levels of institutional security and custody. Their function is to measure risk of assaultive behavior, repeated involvement in prison misconduct, or escape leading to placement in classification levels such as maximum, close, medium, and minimum custody. Such designations are principally used to determine facility assignments and the level of freedom of movement within a prison (e.g., mandatory security staff escort, required physical restraints while being transferred). In other words, the primary function of objective classification systems is to govern interinstitutional transfers to ensure high custody inmates are placed in high security facilities.

Although these systems group inmates according to risk level, within each classification level considerable variation still exists with respect to the inmate's criminal orientation, living stability, likelihood of recommitting crimes, emotional needs, level of education, work skills, honesty, and other factors. Understanding individuals and being flexible in applying different supervision and programming techniques are required to deal effectively with this variety of people and problems. Anecdotal evidence suggests that staff who rely too heavily on one method (e.g., always being controlling or summarily handling all inmates the same) tend to work effectively with some inmates and not others. Staff who develop a better understanding of inmates and use greater flexibility in applying different supervisory and programming techniques may be more effective in managing inmates and controlling prison violence.

Internal Management Inmate Classification Systems

Some prison systems are examining another layer of classification that classifies inmates according to personality typologies (Megargee, Bohn & Sink 1979; Quay 1984). These systems are designed to complement objective custody classification systems. Their task is to classify inmates who share a common custody level (minimum, medium, close, or maximum) according to their personalities and then devise unique housing and program interventions for such inmates within a specific prison facility.

Quay's (1984) Adult Internal Management System (AIMS) is one of the first and best known internal management classification systems. It has been implemented in a few facilities in the Federal Bureau of Prisons and a number of state systems. AIMS relies on two inventories to classify inmates: (1) the analysis of life history records and (2) the correctional adjustment checklist. Each inmate is assigned to one of five groups based on responses to the two inventories. It has been found that for each group, there is a different expected rate or frequency of misconduct. For example, AIMS groups one and two are characterized as "heavy," meaning that they are likely to be management problems and become involved in aggressive, assaultive, or manipulative behavior. AIMS group three members are better behaved and pose "moderate" management problems, while AIMS groups four and five members are "light" or minimal management problems. Groups one and two are further characterized as victimizers and hostile to authority, and groups four and five are characterized as easily victimized. Accordingly, it is wise to separately house these groups to avoid the potential for victimization of inmates from groups four and five from inmates classified in groups one and two.

An evaluation of AIMS conducted by Quay (1984) was published by the American Correctional Association. The evaluation design was a somewhat unorthodox quasi-experimental time-series design involving unmatched control and experimental facilities. A maximum security federal penitentiary (referred to as the "target" institution) was selected as the test site for AIMS. At that facility all inmates were classified according to AIMS and placed in one of three separate housing units commensurate with the major AIMS classification typologies (heavy, moderate, and light housing units). It was hoped that by separating inmates in this manner and training staff in how to respond to inmate situations, prison violence would be reduced.

To test the effect of AIMS, Quay compared the frequency of assaults occurring at the AIMS facility with that occurring at other federal facilities. Frequencies of inmate assaults on staff as well as inmate assaults on inmates at the AIMS prison (target) were compared with four other federal prisons for the year before AIMS implementation (pre-AIMS) and for four years after AIMS was implemented (post-AIMS).

Because the "control" prisons were of different population sizes, the average size of the smallest prison was taken as a base (100), and the size of the other prisons was presented as a multiple of that base. The AIMS prison was the largest of the five prisons, with a base rate more than two and one half times larger (255) than that of the smallest prison. Quay calculated the expected rates of assaults proportionately based on the population percentage and the total number of assaults that occurred at all five prisons. Thus, the AIMS prison was expected to have 27 percent of the assaults each year, while the other prisons were expected to have the remaining 73 percent of assaults.

Although the reported findings indicated that separation of inmates by AIMS resulted in significant reductions in both staff and inmate assaults for three of the four years analyzed, the somewhat unconventional methodology used by Quay leaves many questions unanswered. For example, unless assignments to each of the five institutions were totally random, basing expected assault rates solely on the proportion of population housed at each facility may not be valid. Although actual assault rates were certainly lower than the "expected" rates at the target facility, comparisons of actual numbers yield less dramatic results: in the year prior to use of AIMS, 19 assaults on inmates were reported; in the four years in which the system was used, assaults on inmates averaged 17.5 per year. Data regarding assaults on staff are somewhat more impressive. Although the number of assaults on staff increased dramatically over base year numbers in all four comparison institutions, the number of assaults on staff declined from eleven to an average of eight in the target facility (Quay 1984).

Another study involving separating inmate types was completed in the late 1970s at the Federal Correctional Institution in Tallahassee. Inmates were separated in four dormitory housing units. New inmates and inmates volunteering for drug/alcohol treatment were housed on separate sides of dorm A in the admission/orientation center and the drug/alcohol treatment program. Likely predators and overflow general population were housed in dorm B. Likely victims and overflow general population were housed in dorm C. The general population was housed in dorm D. The study showed that this separation of inmates based on typologies derived from a combination of Minnesota Multiphasic Personality Inventory scores, AIMS correctional adjustment checklist inventory, and record reviews resulted in significant decreases in the number of assaults on staff and other inmates (Bohn 1979). Furthermore, other serious infractions (those referred to disciplinary committees) declined from 315 during the nine-month premanagement classification system period to 289 for the first nine-month follow-up period and 244 for months ten through eighteen (Bohn 1981).

However, there appears to be some significant methodological problems with Bohn's analysis. First, the design is a pre/post test with no comparable control group. Observed declines for the two nine-month follow-up periods could be attributed to a number of external factors unrelated to the classification system. Second, closer examination of the data indicates that nearly all of the reduction in violence is attributable to the general population ("average") inmate group. Other groups remained virtually unchanged. Nevertheless, separation of average offenders and victims from potential predators offers promise in enhancing safety and in efficiently allocating staff resources to those requiring the most supervision.

Prisoner Management and Client Management Classification Systems

The Prisoner Management Classification (PMC) system also groups inmates into typologies designed to provide staff with a mechanism to quickly identify potential predators and victims as well as inmates requiring special programming or supervision. PMC was developed independently from AIMS and other internal management systems.

It was adapted from Client Management Classification (CMC), an offender management system originally developed for probation and parole in the late 1970s. CMC has become a widely used case planning and offender management system in probation and parole. CMC training has been supported by NIC since 1980, and it is estimated that, nationwide, 8,000 to 10,000 officers and workers have been trained in the system.

Three significant evaluations of the CMC process have been undertaken to date. The first was undertaken in 1979 by System Sciences Inc., in Milwaukee, Wisconsin, comparing differences in three outcome measures: probation revocations, full-time employment, and income. Probationers classified as high risk by the Wisconsin risk assessment scale were randomly assigned to one of three groups:

- regular supervision

- intensive supervision, which required increased staffings, referrals, and client contacts

- CMC/intensive supervision, which consisted of increased

staffings, referrals, and contacts combined with CMC assessments and case planning procedures

Results indicate that the CMC/intensive supervision group performed better than the regular supervision group on all three outcome measures (statistically significant at 0.05 level). None of the differences comparing CMC/intensive with intensive supervision or intensive with regular supervision were statistically significant, although the differences were in the predicted direction.

The second study of CMC was conducted in 1985 by the Texas Board of Pardons and Parole. All parolees released from prison in Texas during March and April 1985 were tracked for a six-month period. Forty-six percent of the offenders were supervised by officers using CMC; the remainder were supervised by staff not yet trained to use the system. Although the assignments were not random, the researchers believed that because the trained officers were similar to the untrained officers in experience and demographics, only the area to which an offender returned biased the comparison groups. This study compared regular supervision with CMC supervision of parolees at low-, moderate-, and high-risk levels. The outcome measure used was prerevocation warrants issued at six and twelve months following release. Tests for significant differences indicated that the CMC group performed significantly better than regular supervision parolees overall and at the high- and medium-risk levels.

The most impressive results of any evaluation of CMC conducted to date were reported by the South Carolina Department of Parole and Community Corrections (McManus, Stagg & McDuffie 1988). Matched samples of probationers, one group supervised using the CMC system, the other supervised under agency standards without CMC, were followed until termination. Outcomes reported for the CMC group were significantly better (14.6 percent return rate to prison) than those reported for the comparison group (38 percent return rate to prison). However, questions regarding the sampling methodology were raised that suggest that control populations were not truly equivalent, thus limiting the evaluation's validity. Nonetheless, the results of the South Carolina study are consistent with the other studies and, when coupled with Wisconsin and Texas results, adds credibility to the view that CMC can have positive effects on probation and parole outcomes.

CMC has spread in recent years to various types of residential and nonsecure correctional facilities in Utah, Vermont, and Wisconsin. In 1987, the Correctional Services of Canada began using CMC for case management and programming purposes in all prisons and parole offices throughout that country. However, the Washington experiment represents the first time that it has been used to separate inmates for housing and unit supervision in a secure facility.

Prisoner Management Classification

In a secure prison facility, PMC assignment is determined by a forty-five-minute interview with the inmate conducted by a specially trained classification officer. The semistructured interview consists of forty-five attitudinal items that deal with the inmate's attitudes regarding the instant offense(s); criminal history (including juvenile criminal history); relationships with family, staff, inmates, and peers; current difficulties (psychological, sexual harassment, etc.); and plans after release from prison. In addition, there are eleven factual ratings of the inmate's social status and offense history, eight ratings based on the inmate's behavior during the interview itself, and seven ratings of the interviewer's impressions of the inmate's most and least important problem areas. Responses are coded by the interviewer using a forced-choice rating system and then tallied to reach a PMC classification. Inmates are classified into one of the five PMC categories that attempt to group inmates along a variety of dimensions reflecting criminal sophistication, attitudinal development, and institutional needs.

Selective Intervention-Situational and Selective Intervention-Treatment Groups

Both selective intervention-situational (SI-S) and selective intervention-treatment (SI-T) groups are characterized by a generally positive, social value structure and stable lifestyle. For SI-S inmates, the criminal offense history is usually limited, with the current offense often being the first. Criminal conduct is generally the result of an isolated stressful event. As such, criminal behavior is at variance with the individual's usual value structure. SI-S inmates generally have no special programming or supervision needs.

The SI-T group is differentiated from the SI-S group by the presence of one or more of the following specific factors: sexual offense history, serious drug or alcohol abuse, serious emotional disturbances, or assaultive offense history. These inmates present specific and chronic emotional/psychological problems that are likely to continue without program intervention. Although frequently able to function vocationally and interpersonally, the likelihood of continued criminal involvement is great unless psychological needs are handled appropriately before release.

Both of these inmate types tend to present the fewest problems, tend to make good use of insight and reality-oriented counseling, and usually are more honest and reliable in their reporting than the other PMC groups.

In the institution, SI inmates may experience excessive sensitivity about their crimes and about incarceration. Depression may occur, especially during the early stages, and may include suicidal thoughts and extreme swings from self-blame to denial of all responsibility. Intense withdrawal may be followed by equally intense attachments to other inmates. If these attachments become sexual, fears about sexual identification may result. Relatedly, attachments may form to criminally oriented peers. This may be the result of the SI inmate's perceived need for protection or acceptance and will often result in exploitation by more criminally oriented or sophisticated peers.

The initial isolation of SI inmates may be increased by harassment by other inmates who perceive them as overly conforming and exhibiting superior attitudes toward others in the population. Until personal stability is restored, adjustment to the institution may be difficult, and conduct problems may occur. Over time, SI inmates often adapt well to the institution setting, presenting the fewest security problems and providing a positive influence in the housing unit.

Casework/Control Group

The casework/control (CC) group is characterized by chronic and generalized instability, often the result of chaotic and abusive childhoods. In adulthood this instability may be manifested in drug abuse, frequent changes in residence and employment, and attachment to others who are equally unstable. Emotional problems are frequently evident. Periods of depression may result in suicide attempts and/or hospitalization. In the institution, the CC group frequently encounters interpersonal problems with other inmates and with staff. Authority problems and generally negative responses to others will often result in institutional misconduct. As with the criminal behavior of this group, prison misconduct may range from the trivial to the serious and is often the result of chemical, emotional, or interpersonal problems. Drug trafficking may occur, as well as attempts to secure prescription medication through the manipulation of other inmates or clinical/medical staff.

In the housing unit, CC inmates can cause considerable disruption. Their interpersonal problems and negative attitudes often result in difficulties with cellmates and frequent requests for cell changes. When friendships are formed, they are often inappropriately intense, possessive, and short-lived. Problems in the housing unit may also include generalized intolerance and demands for unearned privileges.

Environmental Structure Group

The environmental structure (ES) group is characterized by a lack of social and vocational skills. These individuals are often easily led and frequently encounter criminal difficulties through association with more criminally oriented and sophisticated peers. Intellectual deficits can be found in this group and may contribute to the general lack of social, vocational, and survival skills.

Their involvement in crime is generally impulsive and unsophisticated and is frequently motivated by a desire to be accepted by others. Although their behavior can be dangerous and assaultive, their motivation is seldom malicious. More often, their behavior displays a lack of insight and a strong dependency.

Prison staff should expect difficulty in working with ES inmates given their lower intellectual and aptitude levels. Prison routine and individual work responsibilities should be explained slowly and simply. Repetition is essential with ES inmates because they are usually unable to generalize from one situation to another. ES inmates will often form attachments to prison staff who are accepting and supportive. This can be used positively and can be helpful in limiting the influence of exploitative inmates on ES inmates.

Security problems with ES inmates are generally related to their impulsiveness and their exploitation by others. Their intellectual deficits can result in a basic lack of understanding of institution rules and routines. These inmates are seldom adept at dealing directly with specific problems or constructively with interpersonal conflicts.

In the housing unit, prison staff should be aware of the susceptibility of ES inmates to manipulation and exploitation by others. They are often motivated by a desire to be accepted and have difficulty differentiating between positive and negative influences. Cell assignments should, where possible, place these inmates under the influence of positive and supportive inmates and staff.

Given the likelihood of intellectual as well as skills deficits, ES inmates frequently have difficulty being accepted as equals in the housing unit. They are often perceived as slow, odd, and unsophisticated. Except when they are used and manipulated by others, they frequently experience isolation. A supportive stance by staff can be helpful during the initial period of confinement until the ES inmate is able to locate a more accepting and tolerant inmate peer group.

Limit-setting Group

The limit-setting (LS) group is characterized by a strong, well-developed criminal orientation and a general lack of commitment to social values. These individuals often appear motivated toward success in crime and have little interest in applying their skills or talents to socially acceptable endeavors. Criminal behavior within this group is generally motivated by money, excitement, and power. Criminal histories are often lengthy and marked by numerous felonies and violent or aggressive offenses. LS inmates are often well-known to the criminal justice system and are often quite comfortable in correctional facilities. Among the LS population, self-concept is often strong and positive. There appears to be a strong degree of professional pride in criminal activity and in "beating the system." Although chemical abuse may be present, it is often a by-product of the inmate's criminal lifestyle and environment rather than a primary motivator.

LS inmates may adapt well to institutions because of previous involvement with the criminal justice system and a well-developed ability to manipulate a familiar environment. These inmates may dominate the more desirable jobs and/or program placements. Program achievement, however, may not be indicative of real change in attitude. Behavioral expectations in the institution must be clearly stated and consistently enforced. Testing of limits should be anticipated. All violations, even minor, should be met with fair and consistent sanctions. Leniency is generally perceived as weakness by these inmates, while fair and consistent use of power can, over time, foster respect.

LS inmates often emerge in a leadership role within the inmate power structure. Impressionable or vulnerable inmates should be protected from this group.

Housing and Programming

Once classified, guidelines suggest how staff should house the inmate and conduct supervision and programming. Specifically, PMC is designed to produce the following housing and program interventions:

- house inmates according to their PMC-defined classification.
- apply specialized supervision in each PMC-defined housing unit using PMC inmate management guidelines.
- use PMC to determine appropriate placement in counselling and other institutional programs.

The major assumption is that if these primary goals are realized, one could then expect improvements in the safety and well-being of the inmate population and institutional staff.

Research Design

To measure the effectiveness of PMC in terms of improving the overall operations of a prison facility and reducing the risk to safety of staff and inmates, the National Council on Crime and Delinquency (NCCD) conducted a study for the Washington Department of Corrections (DOC), funded by the National Institute of Justice (NIJ). The study used an experimental design where inmates were randomly assigned to either the Clallam Bay Corrections Center (CBCC) using the PMC system (experimental group) or other prisons using traditional classification systems (control group). CBCC and the control prisons were medium security prisons.

Other research designs were implemented to supplement the experimental research methods. Time-series analysis was conducted to compare the aggregate levels of misconduct occurring at CBCC with that at similar facilities within the DOC. A process evaluation was conducted to assess implementation of PMC and its operations at CBCC. Interviews and questionnaires were administered to staff at CBCC and other facilities to determine how well CBCC staff accepted the PMC system and to learn how it compared with other management methods being used elsewhere. In sum, a variety of research methods were used to both describe the implementation and operation of PMC and to evaluate its relative effect on inmate behavior, staff acceptance, and other measures of correctional operations.

Experimental and Control Group Design

The core of the study was a comparison of the experimental and control groups, based on a random sample of 488 medium custody inmates ad-

Table 1		
Characteristics of Experimental and Control Groups		
	Experimental (N=243)	Control (N=245)
Race		
White	65.0%	64.1%
Black	22.2%	20.0%
Other	12.8%	15.9%
Age (mean)	30.0 years	30.0 years
Minimum Sentence*	4 years 10 months	4 years 11 months
Violent Offender	69.2%	73.8%
Commitment Offense Type		
Person	49.0%	46.5%
Property	19.8%	17.1%
Sex	21.4%	27.3%
Drug	8.6%	8.6%
Other	1.2%	0.4%
Initial Classification Level		
Segregation	0.0%	1.2%
Mental Health	0.0%	0.4%
Close	3.4%	10.2%
Medium	96.2%	77.0%
Minimum Restrictive	0.0%	4.1%
Minimum	0.4%	4.5%
Intensive Custody	0.0%	2.5%

Excluding inmates with life sentences.

mitted to the DOC from September 1987 to September 1988. During this time period, the DOC was maintaining a prison population of 6,785 inmates throughout its various prison facilities, of which 3,814 (56 percent) were classified as medium security by the DOC's objective custody classification system. (Shortly after admission, inmates are classified into four security levels: maximum, close, medium, and minimum.)

Inmates assigned to medium security level at intake who met specific eligibility criteria were randomly assigned to CBCC, a newly constructed 571-bed, medium security prison that served as the experimental site of the study. Eligibility criteria were as follows:

- initially classified as medium at admission

- not specifically targeted for treatment in the state's sex offender program

- not actively psychotic

- sentence length between two and nine years (minimum sentence length for eligible inmates was later reduced to eighteen months)

- not developmentally disabled

- no medical needs of such severity that CBCC could not handle

The random assignment process enabled an experimental group and a control group to be established to directly test the effect of PMC. (It must be noted that this experimental design was flawed in that it was unable to control the effects of the CBCC facility architecture. CBCC was a new facility with state-of-the-art design. Consequently, the observed effects between the experimental and control populations may be an artifact of facility design or the net result of facility design and PMC.)

The control group was classified using the PMC instrument but was not managed according to PMC guidelines. This was done for two reasons: (1) to ensure that the control group was equivalent to the PMC experimental group by comparing results from PMC classification and (2) to validate the PMC instrument using inmates who have not been "contaminated" by being handled according to PMC guidelines. Observed differences in inmate behavior between the two groups could then be attributed to the classification system experimentally applied to the test subjects.

Comparisons of the Experimental and Control Groups

Equivalency between the experimental and control groups was tested by comparing demographic variables. Results show that the two groups are statistically equivalent (see Table 1 on page 82).

Both groups were predominantly white (65 percent), with about one-fifth black. The mean age was thirty years, and the minimum sentence length was close to five years, after excluding those with life sentences. Almost three-fourths of the inmates were classified as violent offenders. Close to half of the inmates in both groups were serving time because they had committed a crime against person.

The majority of the sample inmates were single: 46 percent of inmates were never married, and 26 percent were either separated or divorced. Two-thirds of the inmates had not finished high school and one-fifth had attended some college or equivalent. Seventy-eight percent of all inmates had committed at least one prior offense, and 68 percent had been previously imprisoned for at least one year. Over half had their first court appearance before age eighteen. Last, 70 percent of these inmates had served probation or parole terms of a year or more.

One variable showed a significant difference between the experimental and control groups: classification level. Almost all inmates (96 percent) sent to CBCC were initially classified as medium compared with only 77 percent of the control group. This is attributable to the fact that although all control inmates were all initially classified by reception staff as medium, there was an opportunity for reception staff to alter this initial classification designation prior to transfer to non-CBCC facilities. Such an opportunity was not afforded the CBCC experimental cases because there was pressure to quickly fill the newly opened CBCC facility. In essence, the security level for the control population reflects the fact that some portion of the experimental cases also were not medium security and would have been so designated were it not for the experimental study.

Implementation

The implementation of PMC at CBCC affected many of the major aspects of prison operations, including housing, inmate supervision, programming, and case planning. Organizing CBCC according to PMC was a major developmental effort affecting staff at all levels. It required a strong administrative commitment to PMC concepts, training, operational changes, and supervisory oversight of staff to ensure that the concepts were correctly implemented and consistently applied.

Implementation required much more than conducting the PMC interview and assigning a PMC typology to the experimental group inmates. The assigned PMC typology needed to guide housing decisions, inmate supervision, and programming. Indeed, the true test of successful PMC implementation is the extent to which PMC is used in these other areas and the extent to which its use is deemed helpful.

CBCC was chosen as the test site for PMC principally because it was a new prison. Because PMC represents a significant departure from conventional operations, it was thought that staff acceptance of the concepts might be greater at a new prison with new staff and newly developed methods of operation. CBCC consists of six separate housing units. PMC places inmates into one of three housing units, each holding 109 inmates. Unit A houses casework control (CC) inmates, Unit B houses both environmental structure (ES) and selective intervention (SI) inmates, and Unit D houses limit setting (LS) inmates. Unit C is designated as a "general population" unit, housing overflow population that cannot fit into the other units. Unit E houses both segregation and initial reception inmates, and Unit F houses the transition population. As room becomes available in one of the three PMC units, PMC-scored inmates from the transition unit are brought in to fill vacancies. The purity of the PMC housing units increased steadily. At the time of the study, 88 percent of the inmates in Unit A were CC, 82 percent in Unit B were ES/SI, and 95 percent in Unit D were LS.

In addition to housing assignments, counselors, program staff, and educational staff were to consider an inmate's PMC type when making case management decisions. The PMC case handling guide was to be used by staff to aid in making the most appropriate programming decisions and in preparing formal, written case plans for inmates. This guide also suggests intervention approaches that work best for inmates based on their PMC type.

The security/uniformed staff in the housing units were to use the case handling guide to impose differential forms of supervision when responding to disturbances in the unit and just generally dealing with inmates on a day-to-day basis. Although there were individual differences among inmates of the same PMC type, CBCC uniformed staff reported that each of the PMC housing units had taken on distinct "personalities" consistent with the descriptions of the PMC type. They reported that using different styles of interacting with inmates based on PMC guidelines helped them manage the prison population more safely.

Staff Reactions to PMC

PMC represents a sophisticated approach to the management of inmates in a prison environment. To succeed, it requires a staff well-trained in its use and supportive of the overall approach. As staff exude greater confidence in the prison's internal management system, staff morale and performance are also likely to improve. Thus, an important component of the evaluation was to determine the level of support for PMC by CBCC staff.

To address these issues, CBCC staff and staff of the four control facilities were asked to complete a voluntary survey. Sixty-four CBCC staff and 172 staff from the control facilities responded. Respondents included administrative, classification/program, and security staff in the housing units. The CBCC survey focused on staff perceptions of whether PMC was helpful as an inmate management tool. Responses to general questions posed to both CBCC staff and staff from the other prisons were compared to determine if significant differences were present among facilities in the state.

Table 2 presents CBCC staff perceptions of PMC. This information indicates that staff believe the PMC scoring instrument provides an accurate classification of the inmate and that it is an improved method for supervising inmates. Staff confirmed by an overwhelming margin (84 percent) that actual inmate behaviors were similar to the predicted descriptions of each of the five PMC types. Seventy-five percent of the staff also felt that PMC was better than previous methods for conducting housing unit supervision of inmates. The survey also confirmed that the LS and the CC housing units, which contained inmates projected to be the most problematic, were indeed the most problematic. Conversely, the ES/SI unit was cited by staff as presenting the least amount of problems. These results mirror anecdotal statements of staff during implementation and are verified by the misconduct rates of each of the PMC types.

The survey verified what was widely reported during implementation: PMC was not being used by counseling or program staff for making program assignments. This was a result of CBCC being a new facility with many programming options not yet fully operational. The DOC has since made a concerted effort to ensure that counseling staff use PMC guidelines when making programming decisions. The fact, however, that PMC was not being used for structuring program assignments according to inmate needs during the study resulted in an evaluation of the effectiveness of separate housing and supervision according to PMC guidelines and not an evaluation of the PMC system as a whole, as was originally designed.

Staff attitudes toward inmate housing and prison safety were assessed at CBCC and the other prisons. CBCC staff were of the opinion that inmates were being placed in the most appropriate housing unit (65 percent indicated "most of the time" and 32 percent said "some of the time") and agreed that housing assignments were made in what they considered to be a fair and consistent manner (87 percent strongly agreed or agreed). However, staff from the other prisons also were generally satisfied with their non-PMC housing assignment processes. Sixty-two percent of the staff at the other prisons were of the opinion that inmates were placed in the most appropriate housing unit most of the time, while 31 percent indicated "some of the time." Eighty-one percent were of the opinion that housing assignments were made in what they considered to be a fair and consistent manner.

Table 2 Staff Perceptions of PMC Inmate Behavior and Management			
	Yes (%)	No (%)	Unknown (%)
Are inmate behaviors similar to the description of their PMC type?	84	12	4
Is PMC better than previous methods for supervising inmates?	75	14	11
Is PMC used for programming decisions? (Classification/Program respondents only)	0	57	29
Ranking of housing units with the most problems in order of severity			1: LS Unit 2: CC Unit 3: GP Unit 4: ES/SI Unit

Similar results were observed on the key question of whether PMC helps staff manage the inmate population more safely. While more than 82 percent of CBCC staff respondents felt that PMC contributed to greater safety in the prison, a similar percentage (80 percent) of staff at the other prisons felt that their system contributed to greater safety as well. Collectively, the survey results suggest that while PMC is well-accepted by CBCC staff and is believed to be an effective system that provides a safer environment, it does not generate higher levels of staff acceptance and support when compared with traditional classification and management systems.

CBCC and the other prisons report similar rates of job satisfaction, with three-fourths of all staff indicating they are either very satisfied or satisfied with their job situation during the previous six months. CBCC staff reported a greater level of moderate job stress while staff at other prisons reported less job stress. The higher level of stress reported at CBCC may be related to the unique pressures associated with opening a new facility with new staff. About 60 percent of CBCC staff reported that PMC does not affect their level of job satisfaction or stress. About one-third reported that PMC increases their job satisfaction and reduces stress. No one reported less job satisfaction with PMC, and only 10 percent reported that PMC leads to more job stress. There were no major differences between the CBCC and other prison staff on these measures of job satisfaction and stress.

In summary, PMC has face validity at CBCC to most administrative, supervisory, and line staff. The concepts and methods of PMC made sense to most CBCC personnel and were deemed helpful in operating the prison and managing the inmate population effectively and safely.

Observed inmate behavior corresponded to the descriptions of inmates' PMC types. Inmates in the CC and LS housing units reportedly presented the most problems. Separating the ES/SI types from the CC and LS types also was reportedly desirable from a case management perspective. PMC guidelines were deemed especially helpful by housing unit staff. PMC had less than the expected effect on programming. However, it was clear that CBCC staff perceived that the greatest benefit of PMC is its use for housing separation and day-to-day unit supervision. The positive staff perceptions are significant because it clearly indicates that PMC can be successfully applied in a secure prison setting.

The Effect of PMC on Institutional Violence and Misconduct

A key question of the research was whether placing inmates in unique housing units and supervising them according to the typological guidelines provides any measurable effects on individual inmate behavior or on the institution as a whole. The study sought to answer this question in three ways. First was an examination of the differential rates of misconduct for the experimental and the control groups to see if CBCC inmates performed better than inmates placed in traditional prison management systems and institutions. Next was an examination of whether official measures of inmate misconduct vary according to PMC typologies, looking for evidence that PMC does indeed provide for accurate classifications and whether the PMC management model is most effective with certain inmates. Finally, time series trends were examined to determine how the aggregate rates of misconduct and program participation at CBCC compared with the control facilities'.

Experimental and Control Group Infraction Rate Comparisons

The infraction rate is defined as the percentage of inmates who have committed one or more major infractions during the first six months after admission to their designated facilities. Only inmates who either had been at CBCC for at least six months of continuous confinement (the experimental group) or had been continuously confined for six months in other facilities (the control group) are reported here to ensure the time at risk for infractions is equal for both groups.

Using the measures of major infractions and the most serious of the major infractions (called "serious major"), statistical comparisons were made between the experimental and control groups. As shown in Table 3, the PMC inmates performed better than the control group on both measures of major and serious major infractions. The differences in commission of serious major infractions approaches statistical significance at the 0.07 level for the chi-square test and is statistically significant at the 0.001 level for the T-test. Although these differences are moderate, both suggest that the CBCC inmates are performing better than the control inmates. And, considering how infrequently serious major infractions occur, any significant reduction over a six-month time period would be difficult to achieve.

Variations in Inmate Misconduct by PMC Level

PMC instruments identify SI and ES inmates as the weaker and less troublesome inmates and CC and LS inmates as the more dangerous inmates. One would expect, therefore, the CC and LS inmates to experience higher levels of misconduct than SI and ES inmates. Levels of misconduct for these four groups were studied to better understand differences observed in Table 3.

Table 3						
Infraction Rates by Experimental and Control Groups (State Inmates Only*)						
Infractions	**Experimental** (N = 23)		**Control** (N = 245)		chi test	t-test
	%	Mean	%	Mean		
Major	38.7	0.89	43.8	0.98	p = 0.24	p = 0.003
Serious Major **	7.6	0.08	12.4	0.14	p = 0.07	p = 0.001

*At the time of the experiment, Washington was renting space to the federal system. Since this was only a short-term situation, federal inmates were not included in the above analysis.

**Serious major infractions include assault resulting in hospitalization; possession of weapons; possession of narcotics, intoxicants, or paraphernalia; possession of staff clothing; rioting; and inciting a riot.

In looking at infraction rates of each PMC type (Table 4), as expected, CC and LS inmates in the experimental group posed more problems to the prison system than inmates in the SI/ES group. Sixty percent of the CC group and 54 percent of the LS group demonstrated misconduct compared with 25 percent in the SI/ES group.

To test the effect of housing inmates according to their PMC type, infraction rates of the experimental and the control groups by the four PMC types are also compared in Table 4. Within the control group, infraction rates do not vary significantly among the different types of inmates. When infraction rates are compared by PMC types across the experimental and control groups, segregation has a limited effect in reducing misconduct. Although the SI/ES group performed better in a PMC environment, neither CC nor LS inmates showed any improvement in behavior when segregated. In other words, PMC benefits inmates who cannot protect themselves from predators but, at best, seems to only contain and not reduce misconduct in more aggressive inmates.

	Experimental				Control			
	Major %	Mean	Serious Major %	Mean	Major %	Mean	Serious Major%	Mean
SI/ES	25.0	0.71	2.7*	0.03	41.4	.71	10.0	0.10
CC	60.0	0.98	14.0	0.14	45.4	1.42	15.2	0.15
LC	54.0	1.16	13.5	0.16	55.6	1.24	13.3	0.156

Table 4

**Six-Month Follow-Up Infraction Rates
by Experimental/Control Group
by PMC Type
(State Inmates Only)**

Significant at p = 0.01

Time-series Trend Analysis

The final component of the evaluation tested the hypothesis that PMC had a positive effect on CBCC aggregate levels of misconduct as compared with other similar prison facilities. Known as a time-series design, this is a less rigorous quasi-experimental design where problems in measurement and selection may confound the validity of comparing, in this case, CBCC with other facilities. Measurement bias can again occur if different facilities record inmate infractions in a unique and, therefore, unreliable manner.

Aggregate numbers of disciplinary misconduct were collected for a thirty-six-month period from both the control and CBCC facilities beginning in January 1986 and ending in December 1988. These numbers were then converted into rates of misconduct per 100 inmates per month to control for varying facility populations.

Two observations can be made from the data collected. First, the facilities had very similar misconduct rates suggesting that efforts to select equivalent control facilities were reasonably successful. Second, the rates for each control facility were quite stable over the thirty-six-month period indicating that there were no major historical events occurring in the entire Washington prison system that could confound or complicate the comparisons with CBCC.

The rates for CBCC during this same time period were overlapped with a pooled rate for the control facilities. Unlike the control facilities, the rates for CBCC during the first twenty-four months of operations were not stable. There were at least three instances of extreme increases or spikes in the rates. Thereafter, the rates stabilized, and toward the end of the thirty-six-month period the rates dipped slightly below the pooled control prison misconduct rates.

How does one interpret these results? The occasional high spikes for CBCC could be symptomatic of the problems the DOC encountered in opening a new facility. The lower rate reported for CBCC during the last six months of 1988 are consistent with the process evaluation and experimental design results showing that as PMC became more fully implemented at CBCC, more positive results were being achieved during the latter phase of the research. One can further hypothesize that CBCC's misconduct rates may still decline as PMC becomes increasingly used by staff in all phases of program and housing assignments.

Implications

The PMC system is designed to drive housing decisions within a prison and to provide detailed case handling guidelines to assist prison personnel with approaches designed to handle inmates safely and appropriately within the housing unit. Of equal importance, the guidelines highlight programming approaches that should work best with inmates to ensure inmates' prison time is most constructive and beneficial in getting ready for community release and maintaining successful adjustment on release.

Prison staff using PMC require training and oversight when learning and implementing the system. The guidelines provide not only the opportunity, but actually mandate that staff provide differential case handling and programming after housing separation has occurred. Because PMC affects many aspects of inmate handling (housing, supervision, and programming), its implementation should be considered a major organizational development effort.

The implementation experience in Washington indicated that PMC successfully separated inmates and was deemed helpful in identifying and separating potential victims from potential predators. Additionally, housing unit supervision staff welcomed and used the detailed case handling guidelines in conducting PMC unit supervision. Using PMC for programming purposes was the most problematic aspect of implementation, but the difficulties encountered relate primarily to that fact that differential programming options were not fully available at the new prison. Staff acceptance at the administrative, supervisory, and line levels was generally high.

The results of the study showed that separation of the SI/ES inmates from the CC/LS inmates and differential supervision by PMC types resulted in less major misconduct and increased staff and inmate safety. Reductions in major misconduct are improving over time and suggest that PMC has an applied benefit if its use is continued. Because differential programming was problematic during this study, the effect of PMC-driven programming on inmate behavior cannot be assessed at this time. Even with its limited programmatic effect in Washington, PMC exhibits considerable promise as an internal management system, and if used in the future for programming, the results may be further improved.

This study demonstrates that PMC can have an effect in reducing serious misconduct and violence of medium security inmates in a state prison setting. The results of this study indicate that the PMC system can complement objective custody classification systems and increase safety in a prison setting. Innovative approaches to internal inmate management such as PMC offer considerable promise and may be required if prison systems are to effectively deal with increasing population pressures, a greater proportion of violent inmates with lengthy sentences, and greater threats to staff and inmate safety.

References

Austin, J., et al. 1989. *Reducing prison violence by more effective inmate management: An experimental test of the prisoner management classification (PMC) system.* Draft report. San Francisco: National Council on Crime and Delinquency.

Bohn, M. J., Jr. 1979. Classification of offenders in an institution for young adults. *FCI Research Reports*: 1–31.

Bohn, M. J., Jr. 1981. Inmate classification and the reduction of institutional violence. *American Correctional Association Monographs*, Series 1, No. 4. College Park, Md.: ACA.

McManus, R. F., D. I. Stagg, and C. R. McDuffie. 1988. CMC as an effective supervision tool: The South Carolina perspective. *APPA Perspectives* (Summer): 30–34.

Megargee, E. I., M. J. Bohn, Jr., and F. Sink. 1979. *Classifying criminal offenders: A new system based on the MMPI*. Beverly Hills, Calif.: Sage Publications.

Quay, H. C. 1984. *Managing adult inmates: Classification for housing and program assignments*. College Park, Md.: American Correctional Association.

VII. Objective Classification in Tennessee: Management, Effectiveness, and Planning Issues

By Christopher Baird

In September 1984, the Tennessee Department of Corrections (TDOC) contracted with the National Council on Crime and Delinquency (NCCD) to undertake a comprehensive evaluation of the department's inmate classification system. Classification is one of several critical issues addressed in *Grubbs, et al. vs. Pelligrin, et al.*, a suit filed in the Middle District of Tennessee. In an agreement among plaintiffs' counsel, state's counsel, and TDOC, outside evaluators were brought in to analyze department operations in designated areas, including the following:

- management
- inmate jobs
- inmate educational programs
- institutional environment
- security at TDOC facilities
- classification of inmates

In evaluating the department's classification system, NCCD focused on several key issues. In 1982, TDOC adopted the model prison classification system developed by the National Institute of Corrections (NIC). This

The National Council on Crime and Delinquency wishes to acknowledge the cooperation and assistance provided by staff of the Tennessee Department of Corrections. Special thanks go to Howard Cook, director of classification, and Susan Mattson, assistant to the commissioner.

Christopher Baird is senior vice-president of the National Council on Crime and Delinquency in Madison, Wisconsin.

system, with some modifications, was at that time the most widely used classification system in the nation. Although the system offers an excellent base for classification, success in each state remains highly dependent on staff understanding of the system, policies regarding overrides (assigning a classification level outside of the system's guidelines), reclassification, and monitoring processes established to ensure compliance.

The NIC system uses factual background data to determine the "risk" each inmate represents. Offense information, history of institutional adjustment, past escape attempts, and a few stability factors receive numerical weights relative to their overall importance to the classification decision. These "scores" are then totaled to determine the appropriate level of custody. Typically, inmates with histories of violence or serious escape attempts are placed in higher custody levels; nonviolent inmates without histories of major institutional problems receive lower custody ratings.

The first reclassification is completed six months after the initial custody assessment is done. Subsequent reclassifications are completed at twelve-month intervals. At reclassification, less emphasis is given to prior record and more weight is placed on institutional adjustment. Inmates are thus "rewarded" for good behavior, and those with adjustment problems move to higher custody levels. This allows movement between levels for all types of offenders.

When staff disagree with the level of custody recommended by the custody assessment instrument, an override can be requested. Since no standardized classification system can take into account all factors relevant to each case, exceptions or overrides are an important element of all systems. Use of exceptions must be monitored closely to prevent abuse and generally requires the signature of a classification supervisor.

NCCD remained involved in the lawsuit for several years. Periodic meetings were held to reexamine the evaluators' recommendations, assess progress, discuss the department's plans, and negotiate solutions to problems that arose. Through this process, Tennessee systematically implemented significant improvements throughout its correctional system.

In 1991, NCCD was asked by the Select Legislative Oversight Committee on Corrections to again assess the classification system in Tennessee. The primary objective of the second study was to help clarify security requirements for future construction. In combination, the two studies provided a rare opportunity to evaluate a well-designed objective classification system from a number of perspectives.

The issues encountered in Tennessee are not unique. Nearly every corrections department in the nation has struggled with similar problems and few, in the long term, have used classification as well as Tennessee has. Because Tennessee based its system on such a widely replicated classification model, the results of the NCCD analyses should prove instructive to other jurisdictions.

The 1984 Classification Study

The 1984 NCCD study of the Tennessee classification system found that the system in use had little effect on placement decisions and needed substantial changes at nearly every level. Although there existed a basis for an excellent system and NIC classification scales and a well-written user's guide were in place, the system functioned only on paper. Little differentiation existed in the handling of inmates regardless of classification level.

Nearly all inmates (82 percent of the sample) were placed in medium security. Staff throughout the department cited problems with sentencing laws that kept many inmates who were otherwise eligible for minimum security placement at higher security levels. In the NCCD sample, only 31 of 232 inmates (13 percent) initially receiving minimum security scores were actually placed in minimum security settings. However, overrides were found in the other direction as well. Of 109 offenders rated close security at admission, only 11 were actually placed in close security settings; another 5 were placed in maximum security. Eighty-four rated close security were placed in medium; an additional 9 received minimum security placements.

After analyzing these data, NCCD concluded the following:

> To obtain a Close security designation at admission requires a substantial degree of violence in an inmate's history. Mixing these inmates with the general population before a record on institutional adjustment is established puts undue risk on other inmates and staff. Such practices could well result in increased assaults, escapes, and management problems.

> The level of overrides (to both higher and lower security) in the Tennessee Department of Corrections relegates the classification process to a paper system, with no impact on operations. Under such conditions, classification is no longer considered a valuable tool by staff, but simply a time-consuming exercise in futility. It is doubtful that much attention is paid

to proper forms completion making the data collected not only useless, but inaccurate as well.

Lack of information on inmates admitted to the system was also identified as a significant impediment to accurate classification. Three documents were deemed crucial to inmate classification in Tennessee: the presentence report, the jail questionnaire, which summarized each inmate's behavior in local facilities, and the National Crime Information Center (NCIC) arrest report. Of these, only the NCIC report was found with any regularity in files of sample cases. Three other less critical reports are also required by department policy: the local arrest report, the social background report, and the sentence data sheet.

The social background report was completed when a presentence investigation (PSI) was not available. However, this report consists almost entirely of inmate self-reported data and was assessed by the NCCD group to be "inadequate for classification purposes." PSI reports were available for only one of every ten sample cases.

The lack of available information at reception led to an unusually high error rate in classification scores. When NCCD staff rescored a sample of inmates, an error rate of nearly 35 percent was found. These errors in scoring generally resulted in underclassification of inmates, further adding to the risk imposed on other inmates and staff. When inmates were misclassified because of scoring errors, nearly 70 percent were scored at lower levels than they should have been.

Although much of the 1984 study focused on correcting operational problems in classification, one particular analysis had implications for other jurisdictions using the NIC system. Because nearly all Tennessee inmates, regardless of classification level, were placed in medium security, a laboratory situation was, in effect, created. The intent of the classification scale is to correctly identify cases requiring higher or lower levels of security and supervision. Subjecting variously classified inmates to basically identical circumstances provides the opportunity to determine how they behave without the intervening factor of different levels of control.

Of 384 inmates in the NCCD sample who were placed in medium security, 84 scored close custody, 112 scored medium, and 188 scored minimum. Inmates rated close custody and placed in medium had significantly higher rates of infractions reported than inmates who scored medium or lower. Most of the difference was found in A- and B-level infractions, the more serious disciplinary reports.

The 1991 Study

By 1991, TDOC had implemented nearly all of NCCD's 1984 recommendations. Only the recommendation to build classification data into a comprehensive management information system was yet to be implemented. Tennessee used four basic levels of custody: maximum, close, medium, and minimum. Minimum is further broken down into three categories: direct, trusty, and restricted. Placement into each of these minimum categories was based first on scoring at the minimum level and then on policy considerations, most of which center around offense type and length of time until release. General descriptions of each custody level, as published in the department's policy and procedure manual, are presented as follows:

1. Minimum Custody. Inmates in this level require less supervision, although some differing techniques of supervision are needed because of programming and policy restrictions. These are identified as (*a*) minimum trusty—inmates appear to pose the least risk to the community because of such factors as offense conviction or time remaining to serve and have demonstrated an ability to function independent of direct supervision without presenting any management problems, (*b*) minimum direct—inmates appear to pose little or no risk but have not yet been determined to be appropriate for independent work or program assignments, and (*c*) minimum restricted—inmates have demonstrated an ability to function without management problems with minimal supervision but must be housed in a secure facility as relates to offense of conviction, length of time to release, etc.

2. Medium Custody. Inmates in this level are required to be under general supervision and housed within a secure facility. Inside movement (except call-outs) is subject to the issuance of passes. Restraints are required for any outside movement except work or program assignments that require the supervision of armed correctional officers.

3. Close Custody. Inmates in this level, by their conduct and/or offense history, appear to pose a degree of risk to the safety or security of the institution, staff, and other inmates and, therefore, require additional supervision. Attention is directed to the

intended purpose of close custody as adopted from the philosophy of NIC and accepted practice in the field of corrections.

Close custody is reserved for inmates with recent, frequent, and/or severe histories of assaultive and/or escape conduct, which indicates a need for close control.

4. Maximum Custody. Inmates in this level require the greatest degree of control and supervision because of recent and serious conduct directed toward staff and inmates, acts that threaten the security of the institution, or the nature of their sentence or order under which they are committed.

This level includes inmates in administrative segregation as well as in mandatory segregation (e.g., those inmates sentenced to death and those placed on safekeeping status by the court).

The commissioner of corrections and the Select Oversight Committee identified three basic issues to be addressed in the study. They felt the use of the minimum restricted custody level needs to be explored. A large percentage of Tennessee inmates were classified at this level, raising two issues. First, since inmates placed at this level score minimum but have some factor present that results in restriction to a secure institution, it was important to understand why inmates were placed at this level. Second, if these restrictions were appropriate for the vast majority of cases, what housing and staffing requirements were needed to adequately handle the custody needs of these inmates?

Approximately 10 percent of all inmates were classified close custody with the commensurate cost of a single cell and high staff-to-inmate ratio. Inmates were placed in close custody through a variety of means— moving down from maximum custody, from reception based on extreme violence either in the community or while in custody, or through reclassification from lower levels based on poor institutional adjustment or a major infraction. Given the expense involved in maintaining close custody requirements, both the department and the Select Oversight Committee requested a review of this classification category. The issue was: Will additional close custody beds be needed as the population expands, or could some of these inmates function well at lower custody levels?

In conjunction with the close custody issue, questions were raised regarding use of close custody IV—a category that was originally established for "decompressing inmates moving down in custody levels after serving time in maximum." This level was very restrictive and, hence, expensive to operate. Two hundred eighty-eight beds were designated as close custody IV beds, more than what were needed for inmates coming out of maximum custody. As a result, some inmates were placed in this status directly from reception.

The final issue identified was the use of community service centers. In recent years, several problems had emerged. Institutional staff felt that the type of inmate they were getting in minimum security settings increasingly had more serious criminal histories and, therefore, presented a greater risk to the community and the program. The criteria used to place inmates in these settings conflicted with the parole board criteria for release. Therefore, it was felt that inmates were staying too long at minimum. Administrators felt this placed undue stress on both the inmate and the program. Finally, the length of time in the program was affected not only by the parole board but by recent policy changes that allowed inmates within ten years of their release eligible date to be considered for minimum security placement.

Operations

The assessment of operational issues was done primarily through interviews with regional administrators, institutional staff, and classification staff. This information was augmented by data supplied by both the Classification and Research and Planning Sections of the department.

NCCD observations of classification operations are summarized as follows:

1. Despite the lack of automation, the system is well-managed. Considerable attention is given to staff training, and the system is monitored on an ongoing basis by central office staff.

2. The proportion of inmates at each classification level corresponds reasonably well with other states using the NIC classification system, particularly when viewed in the context of each state's crime and incarceration rates.

   It is evident that the high percentages of cases scoring at the minimum level in Tennessee is typical of the experience of other jurisdictions. Evaluations have generally found that increasing the number of inmates at lower custody levels has not resulted in increases in assaults or escapes (NCCD 1985).

3. Although staff at each location had some criticisms of the classification criteria used or weights associated with scale items, references to problems usually centered around individual cases. Some staff felt that, in general, "the scale does not adequately capture past assaultive behavior, cases can move too quickly to lower custody levels, no credit is given for program completion, and more points should be given for past escape attempts."

The issues cited by staff were typical of comments encountered in other agencies using objective classification systems. Although staff concerns should be addressed, they need to be viewed in the context of overall system performance. For example, although concern was expressed regarding the type of inmate coming to minimum security institutions, staff could not cite a corresponding rise in assaults or escapes. In general, the level of assault and escape reported within the entire Tennessee system was quite low, indicating that the classification system was resulting in appropriate placements.

4. The most significant operational "problem" encountered was in the handling of inmates in the minimum restricted category. For the most part, despite their minimum custody designation, they were supervised as medium custody inmates. Two of the three regional administrators agreed that these inmates could function with less supervision, but this was not practical when custody levels are mixed. A facility specifically designated for minimum restricted inmates could be operated at lower staffing levels with less restriction on inmate movement.

If the minimum restricted classification category remained at its current level, this could be an option to pursue. The agency, however, should also investigate the possibility of moving many of these inmates to other minimum categories.

In projecting future bed needs for the TDOC, it made sense, from a classification perspective, to focus the analysis on the minimum restricted category. Although some reduction in the proportion of inmates in close custody beds may have been possible, it was doubtful (given the experience of other states) that significantly fewer than 10 percent of all beds would be needed for close custody. Hence, any savings at this level will be marginal at best.

The minimum restricted category, if handled differently within TDOC, could affect TDOC construction plans significantly. At the time of the NCCD review, fully 30 percent (over 2,500) of all TDOC classified inmates were minimum restricted. The key question is: Why are these inmates who rate minimum on the department's classification form restricted to secure facilities?

Department policy identifies two primary reasons for implementing restrictions: (1) the inmate had over ten years to his or her release eligibility date and (2) the inmate was committed for a serious assaultive offense. Sex offenders, for example, were prohibited from placement at community service centers. Those convicted of particularly violent or notorious offenses may also be appropriately barred from such placement.

An analysis was undertaken to identify (1) reasons why inmates were placed at the minimum restricted custody level and (2) disciplinary report rates as they relate to custody levels. These studies clearly indicated that the number of inmates in minimum restricted could be reduced substantially, that classification scores are truly indicative of the level of problems inmates present, and that minimum restricted inmates have significantly lower rates of disciplinary reports than medium custody cases and, in effect, function like true minimums.

Reasons for Minimum Restricted Status

The NCCD study indicated that 35 percent of all inmates in minimum restricted (MR) status were not within ten years of their parole release eligibility date and, therefore, not eligible for placement in minimum security settings. The remaining 65 percent—nearly 1,800 inmates—were placed in MR for other reasons.

TDOC grouped reasons for MR placement into four major categories:

- criminal history
- inmate behavior
- inmate choice
- limitations by institution

Some of the reasons given for restricting these inmates to secure settings were legitimate. Others, however, were based on factors that were already addressed by the classification system (e.g., disciplinary history) or have a less than obvious relationship to custody needs (e.g., parole violator). Therefore, it seemed that many inmates should be moved out of restricted status and placed in minimum security. A conservative estimate of 50 percent was derived by simply summing the percentages of cases restricted for reasons that could be challenged. The percentage may have been even higher if additional program and job opportunities were available to MR inmates. Some inmates remained in MR status by personal preference; others remained to complete treatment or educational/vocational programs or to retain their jobs. Obviously, programs and jobs are important, and lack of similar opportunities in minimum creates a disincentive to move down the custody ladder. If this situation was remedied, the numbers moving from MR to minimum could approach 60 percent.

Validity of the Classification System

The 1984 study provided an opportunity to compare the behavior of inmates classified to different levels but treated as medium security inmates. The 1991 study permitted a similar study, a review of behavior of inmates classified as minimum but placed in medium security. A review of the disciplinary records of all inmates, regardless of placement was made, and those records were related to classification levels.

The relationship found between classification and disciplinary infraction rates was quite strong (Table 1). The system operated as intended; the results were testimony to both the design and the management of the system. No system, even the best designed, could produce such results without conscientious monitoring and management.

The clear differences in problem behavior among custody levels in this study exceeded any encountered in previous NCCD evaluations. Infraction rates, as well as the seriousness of infractions, increased in accordance with custody levels. The differences in infraction rates reported between cases classified close or maximum and those classified minimum were exceptionally high (over 50 percent). Furthermore, very few infractions committed by minimum security inmates were violent in nature. Hence, the system accurately identifies inmates based on proclivities to cause problems within the institution.

Table 1
Frequency of Disciplinary Infractions by Custody Levels (Stock Population, 4 March 1991)

Classification	All Infractions (%)						
	None	**1-5**	**6-10**	**11-15**	**Over 15**	**Total**	**N**
Maximum	31.1	45.0	13.2	5.7	5.0	100.0	318
Close	27.4	51.8	14.6	4.2	2.0	100.0	809
Medium	42.0	48.9	7.4	1.2	0.5	100.0	2,499
Minimum-Restricted	77.9	21.7	0.3	0.0	0.0	100.0	2,765
Other Minimum	81.1	18.7	0.2	0.0	0.0	100.0	2,103
Unclassified	99.7	0.3	0.0	0.0	0.0	100.0	319
TOTAL	62.9	31.6	4.1	1.0	0.5	100.0	8,813

	Violent Infractions (%)						
Maximum	55.4	39.3	4.7	0.3	0.3	100.0	318
Close	64.5	34.9	0.5	0.1	0.0	100.0	809
Medium	84.2	15.8	0.0	0.0	0.0	100.0	2,499
Minimum-Restricted	96.3	3.7	0.0	0.0	0.0	100.0	2,765
Other Minimum	97.8	2.1	0.0	0.0	0.0	100.0	2,103
Unclassified	100.0	0.0	0.0	0.0	0.0	100.0	319
TOTAL	89.0	10.8	0.2	0.0	0.0	100.0	8,813

Table 1 also clearly demonstrates that minimum restricted inmates behave like true minimum custody inmates and, therefore, require less supervision than medium custody cases. Despite being housed with medium custody inmates, their infraction rate was only slightly higher than the rate recorded for minimum custody cases and considerably lower than that of the medium custody sample. Therefore, the concept of lower staffing ratios in institutions devoted to minimum restricted populations should prove workable.

Planning for New Construction

The implications for future building needs are also substantial. The state has developed projections of inmate populations based on current classification figures.

If it is assumed that 50 percent of all MR inmates who are within ten years of their release eligibility dates could be placed in minimum security settings, the number of minimum security beds needed increases significantly, which should result in a corresponding reduction in construction costs.

Thus, even if several institutions were used exclusively to house minimum restricted inmates (requiring less in staff resources), many minimum restricted inmates remain available to other institutions to perform trusty duties.

Implications

The Tennessee experience is instructive from several perspectives. First, the department found a way to turn adversarial litigation into a vehicle for implementing significant improvements throughout the system. Second, the two classification studies conducted by NCCD clearly indicate the following:

1. A well-designed objective classification system like the NIC model can accurately and systematically identify inmates that represent different levels of risk within institutional settings. Thus, when implemented and monitored properly, such systems provide an excellent basis for safely managing inmate populations. Because the NIC system is so widely used, the Tennessee findings should be of interest to many other departments.

2. Significant proportions of most inmate populations can be housed in low security settings without jeopardizing the safety of the community, institutional staff, or other inmates. Approximately 57 percent of the Tennessee prison population

rated minimum using the NIC classification system. Data regarding subsequent infractions demonstrated that these inmates, as a group, adapt well to prison rules and present few management problems.

3. Construction planning, if driven by classification data, can help states avoid the cost of building more high security beds than are required to safely manage the prison population.

Objective classification systems have assumed a significant inmate management role in many states. The unique opportunity in Tennessee to examine how variously classified inmates behave, without the intervening factor of differences in levels of control placed on inmates, demonstrated that the Tennessee Classification system is an excellent method for classifying inmates and allocating prison resources accordingly.

VIII. Objective Prison Classification Systems: A Review

By James Austin, Ph.D.

Inmate classification systems are designed to determine the level of custody an inmate requires to be safely housed within a prison system. The past decade has witnessed considerable changes in how states make such classification decisions. In the past, states used *subjective* classification systems, which relied heavily on the judgment and expertise of classification staff. The problem with subjective models was the absence of consistency in staff decisions. In other words, the decision-making process became arbitrary and capricious.

To correct this problem, courts and standard-setting organizations, such as the American Correctional Association, recommended that *objective* systems be used. In response, corrections has moved toward objective classification systems that rely on valid and/or reasonable criteria that can be measured in an objective and reliable manner. In general, the variables used for objective classification criteria are factual in nature and have some relationship to assessing an inmate's true risk for conforming to a prison system's rules.

Recent Trends in Prison Classification

Prior to the development of objective prison classification systems in the late 1970s and through the 1980s, classification decisions were largely based on the subjective judgment of corrections professionals who relied on experience and intuition. Although agencies sometimes specified criteria to be considered by classification staff, the relative importance of

James Austin, Ph.D., is an executive vice-president of the National Council on Crime and Delinquency in San Francisco.

each factor was often left to the subjective judgment of each staff person or the unchartered consensus of a classification committee. Such informal criteria may have had little or no relationship to actual prison behavior and, generally, served to perpetuate myths concerning offender conduct.

Moreover, subjective classification systems rarely required much in the way of documentation. It was not possible to measure the classification level of an inmate population nor to assess whether inmates were being housed according to their custody level. The lack of documentation made it impossible to monitor classification system performance or to use classification data for planning future correctional needs, such as staffing, inmate programs, and bed capacity. The lack of accountability and documentation contributed to decisions to inappropriately assign inmates, which, in turn, resulted in increasing intervention by the courts.

The most prominent objections to subjective classification systems can be summarized as follows:

1. *Constitutionality.* Courts have found that entirely subjective methods of placement at initial classification or reclassification are not likely to result in the proper assignments to prevent harm to or by any individual inmate (*Holt v. Sarver*, 309 F. Supp. 362 [1970]; *aff'd*, 442 F.2d 304 [8th Cir., 1971]).

2. *Arbitrariness.* Although a loosely structured system theoretically has the capability to respond to needs on a case-by-case basis, it has the inherent danger of arbitrariness. Because there is little guidance for classification staff, it may be difficult to explain the basis for many placements as other than "gut feelings." Inmates are very likely to perceive the decisions as unfair, and this can lead to frustration (and its potential negative consequences) or to "caseworker shopping" (to acquire the most favorable placement recommendation). Further, arbitrary placement decisions are less likely to result in inmates receiving supervision consistent with their needs.

3. *Inconsistency.* A completely subjective method of placement is especially susceptible to inconsistent decisions. That is, even with the best of intentions, two classification committees may independently arrive at very dissimilar decisions in any given case. Although some variation is acceptable, such a system necessarily impedes meeting the basic objectives of classification and good management.

4. *Validity*. The validity of an instrument is its capacity to measure or predict what it claims to measure or predict. It would be difficult, if not impossible, to test the validity of a subjective classification system. One would not be able to identify the *actual* decision-making components; thus, one could not investigate the effectiveness and accuracy of the classification method (e.g., what factors influenced the classification decision.)

For these reasons, subjective classification systems were increasingly criticized and were viewed as unacceptable in light of court and public demands for accountability in corrections.

The Emergence of Objective Prison Classification Systems

During the 1970s prison systems in the United States became increasingly crowded and dangerous. Sentencing legislation was passed in many states, increasing both the numbers of individuals sentenced to prison terms and the length of sentences for many offenses. Prison populations—already rising—increased dramatically, putting tremendous strain on antiquated facilities originally designed to do little more than house offenders.

One result of these new pressures was a clear recognition of the need to allocate limited physical, program, and financial resources in a manner that best protects staff and inmates while meeting the primary correctional goal of public protection. Classification was seen as a management tool for corrections as well as a means for enhancing consistency and equity in decision making.

Federal court involvement in corrections led many agencies to rethink the relationship between classification and management issues. The court's recognition of the importance of classification to corrections' management was best expressed in *Palmigiano vs. Garrahy* (443 F. Supp. 956, 965 [DRI 1977]):

Classification is essential to the operation of an orderly and safe prison. It is a prerequisite for the rational allocation of whatever program opportunities exist within the institution. It enables the institution to gauge the proper custody level of an inmate, to identify the inmate's educational, vocational, and psychological needs, and to separate non-violent inmates from the more predatory....

Classification is also indispensable for any coherent future planning.

In short, the courts and various standard-setting bodies were pressuring prisons to do a better job of assigning inmates to facilities appropriate to the degree of risk presented by each. To effect such assignments, new methods of inmate assessment, consistently applied throughout the system, were needed.

In addition to court intervention, the need to manage burgeoning prison populations and to project construction needs by custody level demanded valid and reliable classification processes. In response to these various issues and agency needs, objective systems began to be developed in the late 1970s. The first generation of objective classification systems was developed first by the Federal Bureau of Prisons (BOP) and later by the California Department of Corrections and the National Institute of Corrections (NIC).

This first generation of objective classification systems primarily relied on objective and reliable measures of the inmate's offense severity, prior criminal history, family and social stability, and institutional conduct to designate appropriate levels of institutional custody (e.g., maximum, close, medium, and minimum custody). Such designations are principally used to determine facility assignments and the level of freedom of movement within a prison (e.g., mandatory security staff escort, required physical restraints while being transferred, etc.). In other words, their primary function is to govern interinstitutional transfers to ensure, for example, that high custody inmates are placed in high security facilities.

While the BOP classification system and NIC's prison classification model differ in their scoring formats, their use of methodologies to construct their scoring scales and their reliance on weighted factors represented a significant departure from prior classification methods.

Other states, including Alaska, California, Florida, Illinois, Indiana, Michigan, Missouri, New York, North Carolina, Oregon, Pennsylvania, and South Carolina, developed their own objective classification systems that borrow heavily from either the NIC or BOP models.

Expectations of Objective Prison Classification Systems

In switching from subjective to objective classification systems, a number of expectations were articulated that reflected the hope that prison operations would, in general, improve. What follows is a discussion of those objectives that have been most frequently cited in the literature. These expectations often conflict with one another.

Prediction

The early advocates of objective classification believed that it was possible to identify those inmates who were likely to become management problems or escape risks by measuring certain inmate attributes known to be associated with these outcome measures. It assumes that inmates differ significantly in their attributes and that future behavior can be predicted based on inmate attributes. By weighting objective classification risk factors, it was anticipated that the prison system's ability to assign inmates to the most appropriate security level would improve. This expectation was most important for the initial classification decision that relied most heavily on information received from the sentencing court.

Just Deserts

Just deserts is based on creating a system of incentives that encourages inmates to conform to prison rules.

This objective, unlike prediction, assumes that inmate behavior can be influenced by creating a formal system of incentives that rewards inmates for good behavior and punishes for bad behavior. Here, classification is structured to allow inmates to work their way up or down in the system's custody levels based on observed institutional conduct. It recognizes that prediction may be inaccurate and that inmate behavior may change. There must be a mechanism to take into account these circumstances. This objective is best realized via the reclassification process that occurs every six to twelve months and is heavily driven by the inmates' disciplinary and program participation behavior.

Reducing the Potential for Politically Embarrassing Incidents

Although not often formally stated in the literature, a significant goal for objective classification is to reduce and even eliminate the potential for highly publicized escapes or institutional incidents that involve "high profile" inmates. When inmates convicted of notorious crimes or when those who have lengthy criminal records are placed in low security environments and subsequently escape and commit violent crimes or are involved in major institutional disturbances, it can have profound consequences on the tenure of a director of corrections, the governor, and even a presidential election (as the Willie Horton controversy during the 1988 presidential campaign showed). Achieving this objective is often in direct conflict with the objectives of prediction and just deserts.

Organizational Requirements of Objective Classification Systems

Objective classification is more than just a set of scoring instruments. It also requires substantial reforms of existing organizational structures in terms of how inmates are housed and transferred. In particular, objective classification demands a more centralized classification process that limits the ability of institutional staff to determine an inmate's facility placement. In other words, the traditional process of wardens transferring their worst inmates to other institutions and keeping (or hiding) their best inmates from such transfers was ended. All transfers are controlled by the central classification unit as well as approval of local recommendations to override a custody score.

Furthermore, because objective classification systems are complex and automated, they require staff who are specialists in classification. In essence, the classification unit becomes the "brain" of the entire prison system with responsibilities for managing the flow of inmates among the various facilities and/or community programs from time of admission to date of release.

It is now common to find classification divisions staffed by classification specialists at both the central office and facility level whose duties relate exclusively to classification-related activities. Classification systems are now fully automated, greatly enhancing a department's ability to monitor inmate movement and project future resource needs.

The BOP and NIC Classification Systems

Background information on the BOP and NIC classification systems presented here is drawn from a National Institute of Justice report (1987).

The BOP classification system is generally recognized as the first objective prison classification system to be implemented on a systemwide basis. It was initially developed in 1979 after extensive research and testing and was fully implemented at all federal facilities some two years later. It has been evaluated and refined by BOP staff on several occasions and has been adopted by a number of states, including Alaska, Hawaii, Indiana, Michigan, Nebraska, New Mexico, Ohio, and South Carolina.

The NIC prison classification system was developed in 1982 and was widely disseminated by NIC over the next several years. Many states have since implemented the NIC system adapted to local needs with NIC assistance. More directly, as of 1987 the following state prison systems had adopted some version of the NIC system: Colorado, District of Columbia, Idaho, Kentucky, Nevada, North Dakota, Oklahoma, South Dakota, Tennessee, Vermont, Washington, and Wisconsin.

The BOP initial classification form relies on six items to determine a security level designation ranging from security level 1 (SL-1) through security level 6 (SL-6). Each inmate is evaluated on each of these six items and awarded a certain number of points that are then totaled. Based on this point total, the inmate is classified into one of six security levels.

These security level designations are used to indicate the type of facility at which an inmate is eligible to be housed. An initial custody level is also associated with each security level designation. In the BOP system, the custody level refers to the level of supervision over inmates or the restrictions on inmate movement. The level of supervision ranges from the most restrictive (maximum custody) to the least restrictive (community custody), with two intermediate levels of custody in between (in custody and the less restrictive out custody).

Inmates assigned to SL-1 generally receive a community or out-custody designation status. Those assigned to SL-2 through SL-5 facilities begin with an in-custody designation, while those in SL-6 are placed in maximum custody (BOP 1982). For example, maximum custody indicates maximum control and supervision, requiring at least two officers for escorted trips along with the use of handcuffs and leg irons. Maximum custody inmates may also be restricted from participating in work and barred from certain cell assignments. Conversely, inmates classified as out custody do not require external restraints and may work outside the institution's perimeter (BOP 1982).

After being incarcerated for at least six months, the inmate's classification may be reevaluated with a more elaborate custody review form incorporating additional custody factors that place greater emphasis on institutional behavior. A scoring matrix is then used to indicate whether an inmate should be considered for an increase, decrease, or no change in custody level.

The NIC system is streamlined in that its scoring is simplified and uses conventional definitions for custody level (close, medium, and minimum) as opposed to the security levels used by the BOP. Both initial and reclassification forms are used. In the NIC instrument, points are added via a two-step additive scale to determine a custody designation. The initial classification form consists of eight items. The first four items are totaled for each inmate at admission. If the point total exceeds a certain level, then the inmate is classified as close custody. If not, the inmate is then scored on the remaining four items, which involve both the negative and positive points. Based on this score, inmates are classified either as medium or minimum custody.

Like the criteria used in the BOP system, the NIC reclassification form places emphasis on institutional conduct in reclassification. Unlike the BOP system, however, reclassification generally occurs twelve months after initial classification, although some states (e.g., Washington) do a custody review for most inmates at six-month intervals.

Accomplishments of Objective Prison Classification Systems

Despite the need for evaluation, all too few states have undertaken a systematic or rigorous evaluation of their system. The National Council on Crime and Delinquency (NCCD) conducted a survey of all prison classification evaluations completed and published by state prison systems during the past five years (Alexander & Austin 1992). Only eighteen jurisdictions responded that they had conducted such research. Three of these studies (California, Nevada, and the District of Columbia) were instigated by consent decrees that required them to conduct evaluations of classification systems. Several studies were limited evaluations on how proposed objective criteria would affect classification decision making if such criteria were actually implemented. Thirteen states had conducted evaluations on the effect of implemented objective classification criteria. Only one experimental study was conducted. Several studies were severely flawed with respect to extremely small and biased samples.

Despite these methodological weaknesses, the initial evaluations have contributed to a growing body of knowledge on the merits and limitations of objective classification systems as currently designed.

At a process level of analysis, these studies indicate that state correctional agencies and their staffs view these new objective systems as extremely useful in managing their rapidly expanding prison populations. Improvements have been noted in the consistency of decision making by staff, which in turn has increased staff accountability. Override rates are generally well within the 5 to 15 percent range, indicating that staff are generally receptive to the instrument's scoring criteria.

Furthermore, because most of these systems have been fully automated, aggregate classification data can now be used to better plan resources needed in the future, including staffing levels, inmate programs, and types of facilities. Many states, such as California, Illinois, Tennessee, and Nevada, routinely issue population projections based on classification data that heretofore were unavailable.

In terms of system impact, objective classification systems have been found to place more inmates at lower custody/security levels without increasing rates of escape or misconduct. For example, an evaluation conducted by NCCD for the Nevada prison system found that since the implementation of the NIC prison classification system, the proportion of inmates classified for minimum custody has increased over threefold from 8 percent to 25 percent while escapes and serious misconduct reports have declined (Austin & Chan 1985). Similar trends have been reported in Illinois, California, and Alabama (Alexander & Austin 1992; California Department of Corrections 1986).

Studies have also found strong associations between the inmate's scored custody level and subsequent inmate misconduct reports. In other words, inmates who are scored and placed in minimum custody have far fewer disciplinary misconducts than those placed in medium and maximum custody.

Despite this finding, the predictive attributes of the classification system are moderate at best. This is especially true for the initial classification instrument.

One additional finding should be noted based on the California study of its classification system. California found that after having implemented its new system, an increased number of inmates were classified to the lower security levels and rates of violence, escapes, and misconduct, which had been increasing, suddenly leveled off and then actually declined. But researchers also found that inmates who were classified to higher levels of custody but were housed in lower security facilities behaved similar to inmates who were properly housed and classified in lower security facilities. These findings suggested that the prison environment was exerting an independent influence on inmate behavior. In other words, the type of environment as defined by the level of security, staffing levels, program opportunities, and other prison facility attributes may have an equal or even greater influence on inmate behavior than inmate attributes.

The major findings of evaluations completed to date suggest that objective prison classification systems have had the following effects on prison systems:

- Significant decreases in the extent of overclassification. States have found that the proportion of inmates who classify as minimum or lower custody levels is much higher than previously believed. Most states are discovering that 25 to 40 percent of their inmates can be safely housed in minimum custody.

- Increases in the consistency of classification decision making, and decreases in the number of staff errors and misinterpretations of classification policy.

- Decreases or no changes in the rates of escape and institutional misconduct.

- Modest but important improvements in the system's ability to house inmates according to level of risk. While there continue to be difficulties in developing classification criteria that are predictive of risk, there is considerable evidence that current classification criteria do provide a modest, but important, degree of prediction.

- Staff perceive objective classification instruments to be useful tools.

- Despite evidence that inmate misconduct is related to objective classification criteria, there is evidence that institutional environment may be an equal or even more important contributor to inmate misconduct (California Department of Corrections 1986)

The Next Generation of Prison Classification Systems

Despite the achievements, there are a number of issues that need to be addressed by classification approaches to help correctional systems prepare for the future. Prison systems are continuing to expand and are receiving a more diverse offender population. Although the first generation of objective classification systems has proved to be invaluable to prison operations, these additional pressures suggest a need for more refined classification procedures, data, and instruments.

Continued Prison Population Growth and Crowding

Prison populations increased by nearly 150 percent from 1980 to 1991. The operational implications of this rate of growth are obviously enormous. For example, as prison admissions increased in Florida and Texas (two of the nation's largest prison systems), average time spent in prison declined to keep populations within court-imposed limits. The accelerated movement of inmates through the system undoubtedly affected custody, program, and job placements—all basic classification issues (Sharp 1992, Austin 1991).

There has been dramatic growth in the nation's prison population over the past decade, and this growth pattern is likely to continue, although at a somewhat slower rate. The NCCD national prison population forecast now estimates that state prison populations will increase by 35 percent over the next five years.

Further complicating matters is the fact that prison capacity has not kept pace with need. State prisons are, on average, operating at 115 percent to 127 percent of rated capacity. The nation's largest state, California, is a staggering 83 percent over capacity (BJS 1992). Obviously, managing a growing (and changing) offender population under such conditions creates enormous stress on prison resources and increases the importance of a valid, reliable, and efficient classification system.

Implementation Issues

Too often, correctional agencies have naively assumed that objective classification systems can be quickly and easily implemented. Actual experience has shown that it takes at least one year to properly design, pre-test, and implement such a system. Perhaps the greatest obstacles to implementation are organizational in nature. Objective classification is designed to fundamentally alter the process by which inmates are now being assigned to facilities and programs. Consequently, new methods of classification generally threaten existing power relationships within the correctional bureaucracy. Unless the administration at the highest level (i.e., Director or Commissioner) is totally committed to organizational change, any attempts to introduce new classification systems will be resisted and often rejected.

To counteract these forces of resistance, it is critical that the implementation process include the following steps:

1. *Establish a Classification Advisory Committee.* The Director or Commissioner must assign to this committee personnel that not only represent the key functions of the entire prison system (e.g., information services, security, etc.), but the personnel assigned must have the respect of the correctional workforce. They must also have a clear mandate from the Director reflecting her or his goals for classification. Finally, the committee must see this effort as their classification system and not a system that has been "bought off the shelf" from another agency.

2. *Pilot test the system before implementation.* No classification system will work properly unless it has been properly pilot tested on actual inmates. The pilot test requires application of the prototype instruments to a representative sample of the inmate population to learn how well the forms function. More importantly, the pilot test will show the probable impact of the new system on how inmates will be classified and housed once the system becomes operational.

3. *Automate the system.* Classification systems must also be automated. Because they rely on a more sophisticated and structured scoring process, classification systems need to become part of the department's management information system. Automation will reduce errors in scoring inmates for custody level, will better monitor the housing of inmates according

to the classifications system, and will allow evaluations to be conducted on a regular basis to better improve the system's performance.

4. *Provide sufficient staff and training resources.* Classification systems, because they try to centralize the classification process, must rely on a cadre of highly specialized staff who understand the process and can manage the system. In particular, a central office classification unit is required that has overall authority for all classification decisions and inmate movements among the various facilities. Furthermore, because inmate reception and institutional staff will have direct classification scoring responsibilities, a comprehensive training program is needed to ensure a high level of conformity to classification policies and procedures.

5. *Be prepared to monitor and change the system based on evaluation findings.* Finally, all classification systems need to be monitored and periodically evaluated. Monitoring is intended to ensure the system is working as designed. Once that has been verified, evaluations should be undertaken to validate the current system and to determine what impact the system has had on inmate operations and overall performance.

Increased Use of Community-based Placement Options

Largely due to crowding, prison systems are being asked to become increasingly responsible for administering community-based programs outside of traditional correctional facilities. These programs include, but are not limited to, electronic detention, work release, day release programs, and extended furloughs.

As these programs expand, prison officials have to do a better job in determining which inmates pose the least risk to public safety. Traditional prison classification systems are calibrated to assess risk to institutional misconduct and not rearrest while in the community. Consequently inmates who score minimum custody may not be suitable for release to the community. This problem highlights the need to refine existing classification systems so that alternative criteria can be used when making community-release decisions.

Emerging Special Offender and Treatment Populations

Not only are prisons receiving more offenders but their social and offender attributes are also changing. For example, substantial increases in drug arrests over the decade, which has been a major cause of the rapid growth in prison populations, has contributed to increases in prison admissions for women, a population that has grown much faster than the male population (202.2 percent increase for women versus 111.6 percent for men between 1980 and 1989), African Americans, and members of inner city gangs (Bureau of Justice Statistics 1991).

The increase in the number of women incarcerated is important given that most classification systems were developed expressly for male populations. The appropriateness of such application, from both a legal and research perspective is questionable and should be assessed. Because women comprise such a small percentage of the total inmate population (approximately 6 percent), classification issues have received less than adequate attention.

Of perhaps even greater significance is the fact that mandatory sentencing and habitual offender laws, coupled with early release mechanisms designed to shorten length of stay in essence and increases in parole violation rates, have created two prison populations in many states: a short-term offender group that turns over rapidly and long-term inmates, many of whom will grow old and die in prison. The latter group will present significant challenges to existing classification and operational procedures.

Finally, although it does not appear that prisons will soon wholeheartedly embrace a rehabilitative philosophy, emerging trends clearly indicate that treatment programs for special offender groups (e.g., sex offenders, drug addicts, illiterate, chronically unemployed) are receiving renewed emphasis. There is a growing realization that criminal justice sanctions alone have not worked to break the cycle of offending for these groups. Consequently, corrections and classification need to do a better job of identifying those who can best benefit from treatment and ensure they receive such intervention (sex offender and drug abuse programs, education, vocational training, counseling, and/or specialized housing) while the offender is incarcerated.

The Emerging Role of Internal Classification Systems

Decisions at the *institutional* level that guide housing, work, and program assignments need to be as structured and organized as those being made at the *system* level. A second layer of prison classification—internal classification systems—is required.

To help deal effectively with the varying degrees of risk represented by inmates, some prison systems are now beginning to examine another layer of classification that classifies inmates according to personality or behavioral typologies (Megargee et al. 1979; Quay 1984). Some are reasonably well-researched offender typology systems designed by psychologists. Others are simply additional criteria applied by individual institutions to augment the department of corrections' systems. All attempt to address housing, programs, and compatibility issues to improve management at the institutional or facility level.

These systems are designed to complement the objective custody classification (or external) systems referred to earlier. Their task is to classify inmates who share a common custody level (minimum, medium, close, or maximum) according to their personalities, and then devise unique housing and program interventions for such inmates within a specific prison facility. Whereas the objective custody classification models influence interinstitutional placement, the internal management systems focus more on intrainstitutional placement and program assignment.

Recent evaluations of internal classification systems suggest that they can have a positive effect on staff morale and inmate behavior. However, it must also be noted that these are more complex systems that require additional staff training in both inmate assessment as well as interactions with inmates. The fact that so few prison systems have formal internal classification systems in place is suggestive of the care one must take in implementing them. Nonetheless, this second layer of classification will soon need to become part of the next generation of objective prison classification systems.

Conclusion

There has been considerable progress in the past decade in state prison systems moving from subjective to objective classification systems. Because of these systems the level of overclassification has been dramatically reduced without any consequences to institutional or public safety.

Furthermore, states are able to better plan their future prison bed needs and operating expenses based on empirical and sound data.

Despite these dramatic advances, much work still remains. In particular, new classification systems that govern the internal movement of inmates within a facility are required. Prison classification systems also need to better interface with jail, probation, and parole classification systems so that critical information about offenders follows them as they move through the correctional system. And finally, considerable experimentation and research is needed to better understand the influence of the prison environment as it relates to inmate behavior.

References

Alexander, J., and J. Austin. 1992. *Evaluation of the Alabama Department of Corrections' objective prison classification system.* San Francisco: National Council on Crime and Delinquency.

Austin, J., and L. Chan. 1989. *Evaluation of the Nevada Department of Prisons' prisoner classification system.* San Francisco: National Council on Crime and Delinquency.

Austin, J. 1991. *The consequences of escalating the use of imprisonment: The case study of Florida.* San Francisco: National Council on Crime and Delinquency.

Bureau of Justice Statistics. 1991. *Women in prison.* Washington, D.C.: U.S. Department of Justice.

Bureau of Justice Statistics. 1992. *Prisoners in 1991.* Washington, D.C.: U.S. Department of Justice.

California Department of Corrections. 1986. *Inmate classification system study: Final report.* Sacramento, Calif.: California DOC.

Megargee, E. I., et al. 1979. *Classifying criminal offenders: A new system based on the MMPI.* Beverly Hills, Calif.: Sage Publications.

National Institute of Justice. 1987. *Guidelines for developing, implementing, and revising an objective prison classification system.* Washington, D.C.: National Institute of Justice.

Quay, H. C. 1984. *Managing adult inmates: Classification for housing and program assignments.* College Park, Md.: American Correctional Association.

Sharp, J. 1992. *Texas crime, Texas justice.* Austin, Tex.: Comptroller of Public Accounts.

IX. Classification: Its Central Role in Managing the Federal Bureau of Prisons

By Patrick R. Kane

As a matter of history, inmate classification in the United States is nothing new. For more than a century, correctional practitioners have increasingly recognized its value. The founding documents of the American Correctional Association, established in 1870, include ample evidence that even then an accurate inmate classification system was thought to be a worthy goal. Following these precepts over the years, most correctional systems have made attempts at instituting some basic forms of separation—males from females, adults from juveniles, sentenced from unsentenced.

The first comprehensive effort to classify and differentially treat offenders dates at least as far back as 1876, at New York's Elmira Reformatory. There, Zebulon Brockway and his staff set up an entire institution dedicated to the reformation of youthful offenders who had previously been commingled with adults of all ages and criminal sophistication. In those days, that was considered a dramatic, if not radical, strategy for handling convicted criminal offenders.

Classifying Today's Offenders

Today, as we approach the twenty-first century, classification of offenders is a commonly accepted principle. Most, if not all, state and local jurisdictions make some attempt to classify their inmates. The systems in use range from subjective to objective and from simple to complex. But all are based on a general acknowledgment that different categories of offenders

Patrick R. Kane is assistant director, Correctional Programs Division, Federal Bureau of Prisons.

should be separated and treated differently. Most operate on the same set of fundamental premises.

The first of these—explicitly stated or not—is that the best available predictor of future behavior is past behavior. Virtually all contemporary classification systems rely extensively on personal background and criminal history information.

The second premise is that inmates should be held in the least restrictive setting that will ensure public safety and institutional order. To do otherwise is to subject the inmate to unnecessary personal risk and the corrosive effects of association with more hardened criminals and also to incur much higher confinement costs to the agency.

Third, when housed together, inmates tend to present fewer internal management problems if they are confined with similar inmates than if they are housed with those who are more (or less) aggressive or criminally sophisticated.

The final premise—employed by most systems in light of the public safety imperative—is that when in doubt, staff should adopt a conservative posture in making classification decisions.

Goals of Classification

The goals of classification in most adult correctional settings are to ensure public safety, promote efficient inmate management, and enable staff to manage their institutions in a cost-effective manner. In correctional systems experiencing growth, a fourth goal emerges from having a sound classification system: to assist planning staff in determining the type of expanded capacity that is needed, thus ensuring that the types of beds constructed meet the actual security needs of inmates.

Public Safety

The issue of public safety is one that is paramount for correctional administrators: preventing escapes is their number-one priority. Appropriately designed classification systems enable staff to determine the type of institution in which each offender should be confined. Most large correctional systems use their classification structure to guide initial assignments to institutions. In smaller systems with fewer institutional options, classification is valuable in that it allows staff to decide more accurately where inmates are to be assigned when housing units of different security characteristics are used in the same facility. In short, no matter what the size of the system, classification is an essential element in ensuring that inmates remain in custody throughout the terms of their sentences. That important public safety function drives every successful inmate classification system.

Inmate Management

In most prison systems, internal inmate management strategies are based on some form of inmate classification as well, enabling staff to make well-informed decisions on day-to-day operational issues. The classification system assists staff in screening inmates for issuance of gate passes for access to less secure areas of the institution. It can help make appropriate job assignments to areas of the institution or jobs that present higher levels of risk. It assists staff in determining eligibility for escorted trips and furloughs. Classification is the foundation for a great deal of the ongoing management activity in a prison on a daily basis.

Cost-effective Operation

Cost-effective operations result from accurate inmate classification. Construction and operating costs for maximum and high security prison beds are far greater than for those in low and minimum security institutions. Accurate classification enables staff to place inmates in facilities that meet their security and supervision needs, while not overexpending public funds for unnecessarily costly security measures.

Prison Construction and Renovation

The final area where classification can provide significant benefits is in managing prison construction and renovation programs. In years past, many correctional systems initially assigned all inmates to maximum security institutions, where they were screened for housing within that location or for subsequent transfer to a lower security prison, if additional facility resources were available in that system. The result in many systems was that large numbers of inmates were held under unnecessarily stringent, far more costly security conditions. A well-designed classification system enables top administrators and planners to estimate the security needs of the future inmate population and custom-tailor the agency's expansion plans accordingly. By avoiding construction of unnecessary high security beds, the agency promotes the most cost-effective initial construction strategy and avoids the far more costly long-term operating costs associated with high security operations. In a time of rapid expansion of prison capacity across the nation, accurate classification can be a critical factor in controlling expansion costs.

The Bureau of Prisons' Classification System

For these reasons, the Federal Bureau of Prisons (BOP) has adopted a comprehensive inmate classification system that starts at the time of initial assignment to an institution and continues to the time of final release to the community. It is the major screening and guiding factor in a wide range of institutional assignments and decisions throughout an inmate's term. In almost every respect, the BOP's classification system is a highly functional method for accomplishing the four central goals of classification.

But the BOP's current system did not emerge full-fledged from agency headquarters—it is instructive to look at the history of classification in the BOP and the evolutionary development of this system into its present form.

Virtually from the inception of the BOP in 1930, classification has been used to make broad-scale categorizations about its inmate population. Even when the BOP consisted of just three penitentiaries, there was a semblance of classification. At first, the process was crude and highly centralized. It was based primarily on the subjective judgment of the warden or deputy warden, after a cursory interview and a review of whatever records arrived with the offender. Housing and job assignments were the main objective of this process, and there was no appeal; institutional needs and available bed space drove those assignments. Reclassification did not exist as we now recognize it, and inmates were likely to spend their entire sentence in the same status to which they were originally assigned.

With the construction of new medium security BOP institutions in the 1930s and 1940s, more accurate initial assignment options were created for new offenders. Federal Correctional Institutions (FCIs), a medical center, and a reformatory for women were now available for less sophisticated offenders, those with medical or mental health needs, and—for the first time within the BOP—female offenders. This resulted in meaningful designation and redesignation decisions.

During these early decades of the BOP's history, classification committees gradually began to emerge as the prime vehicle for these decisions. Classification committees were typically composed of all institution department heads and were chaired by the deputy or associate warden (usually the one responsible for institutional security). On the surface, every member of the committee had a voice in the inmate's classification. Theoretically, each inmate was to have been interviewed by committee members, and all available records were to have been reviewed, including some basic test scores. However, as a practical matter, the chair held the real authority, and this system merely operated as an elaborate version of the earlier one-person system.

In the early 1970s the BOP began using a series of more organized, rational systems for assigning inmate custody levels. The first such system was called ISM (which stood for intensive, selective, and minimum). This was an early subjective attempt at triage for assigning incoming inmates to programs. A later version, RAPS (rating, age, prior, and sentence) helped staff frame their decisions on program assignments so that inmates who had lower RAPS scores (presumably reflecting amenability to treatment under the medical model) were afforded priority access to limited institutional programs. Although RAPS was implemented bureau-wide, those who used it recognized its limitations. Indeed, the "R" factor represented a purely subjective staff assessment of the inmate's amenability to positive change.

There were other attempts at implementing subsystems for classification in the BOP in the 1970s. The most notable was the Quay system, which separated offenders on the basis of background factors relating to demonstrated aggressiveness and other traits. Although not implemented widely, this system was adopted at the Robert F. Kennedy Youth Center (now FCI), Morgantown, West Virginia; FCI, Oxford, Wisconsin; and the U.S. Penitentiary, Lewisburg, Pennsylvania.

During this same period, through the early and mid-1970s, the BOP was slowly adopting the functional unit management system nationwide. Unit management entails the assignment of a relatively small, interdisciplinary staff to a housing unit, where they provide case management, counseling, and other typical services to inmates in that unit. Unit staff offices are located in the housing area, increasing availability of staff to inmates and also increasing the degree of familiarity of staff with the inmates. The unit correctional officers are members of the team, which is delegated authority for most decisions relating to the inmate's case. This authority includes responsibility for initial and reclassification of all inmates in the unit.

However, with this decentralized approach to management of inmate case decisions, consistency, at times, was an issue. Unit-based classification by staff who were more familiar with each inmate was an improvement, but it also allowed individual experiences and biases of far more staff to come into play. While the classification committee gave a measure of consistency to the overall institutional classification process, the variation in decisions under unit management were significant. As a result, the search for ways to upgrade the RAPS system was coincident with a need to modify the unstructured discretion of unit teams.

In 1977, the BOP commissioned a task force to develop a new, unified classification system for the entire agency. This system was intended to use decision-making elements derived from the professional experience of BOP staff. Once fully developed, it would serve as the basis for initial institutional designation, classification on arrival at that institution, and all subsequent reclassification actions.

The system initially involved an assessment by staff of the following factors:

- expected length of incarceration

- offense severity

- type of prior commitment

- history of violence

- history of escape or escape attempts

- type of detainer

Each of these elements is assessed a predetermined weight and scored on a standard form. In the early years of the system's use, the sum of the points assigned was applied against six numerical ranges that corresponded with security levels. Each inmate was assigned a numerical security level. That level corresponded to an array of similarly numbered institutional categorizations that hinged on the physical security features of each facility and the type of supervision and control they offered. These features included the following:

- type of perimeter

- use of perimeter detection systems

- presence of towers
- use of external patrols
- type of housing unit
- staff supervision levels

Thus, an inmate who scored at the highest end of the security scoring range would likely be assigned to a typical U.S. penitentiary, or perhaps to the U.S. Penitentiary in Marion, Illinois, where the physical controls are the greatest. On the other hand, an inmate scoring in the lowest range of the scale ordinarily would be designated to a minimum security prison camp, with nominal physical controls. Administrative facilities, such as medical and metropolitan detention centers, are designed to hold inmates of all security levels.

No numerically based classification system is infallible—professional judgment still plays a major role in the process. As a result, an important element in this system is ensuring there is a sufficient degree of flexibility, so that staff are able to override the numerically derived security scoring when necessary. Consequently, inmates who might numerically score as qualified for a particular security level institution might still be assigned to a higher or lower level facility, if, based on the considered (and documented) judgment of staff, their background and conduct justified that variation. These management elements were eventually codified in the form of public safety factors, which were then formally considered as part of the classification process.

When an offender is sentenced by a federal judge to a term of confinement, the U.S. Marshal's office for that district makes a request for designation by the BOP. Available factual information about the offender is gathered by the BOP's community corrections manager in that district, who enters relevant data into the BOP's nationwide automated information system and transmits the information to one of the BOP's six regional office designation administrators. That administrator evaluates the incoming background and criminal history information and makes a designation decision based on offender characteristics and security needs, as well as geographic and crowding factors. Inmates with special medical or other treatment needs are designated in accordance with those needs, and whenever possible the BOP honors judicial recommendations as to place of confinement. Although every attempt is made to keep offenders as close as possible to their home communities and families, this often cannot be done because of the need to maintain population balance across the entire federal system.

Once the inmate arrives at the institution, he or she is provided a comprehensive orientation to the BOP's rules, regulations, and programs; physical examinations; educational and other testing; and a series of staff interviews. Initial classification by the unit team takes place within thirty days of commitment and entails a review of all current findings and a recalculation of all of the background factors considered by the designation administrator. Inmates who are found to be inappropriately classified for the initially designated institution are referred to the appropriate regional office for transfer consideration.

At the time of initial classification, and in parallel with this security scoring system, each inmate is assigned a custody classification representing the degree of supervision he or she requires. These were originally stratified as maximum, in, out, and community. While the system correlated security levels and custody, custody assignments were based on additional information, including institutional conduct. This two-tiered structure gives institutional managers needed flexibility in tailoring job assignments and other operational decisions to the inmates they supervise. Thus, there might be inmates in more than one custody level in the same institution.

Once an inmate is classified, regular reviews are a part of the team process and again entail a recomputation of the security designation score that guides institutional assignments. If an inmate's custody score changes significantly (due either to new information about the criminal or personal history or to changes in institutional conduct), he or she may be referred for transfer to an institution of higher or lower security.

The system was tested in representative institutions before being implemented in all BOP facilities in 1979. Every BOP inmate was evaluated on the basis of the new system and assigned a security level score. Population adjustments over time brought the system into balance; inmates were not moved en masse to implement it.

Validation

Validation of any system of this type is important. The decisions made by BOP designators and unit teams affect the lives of many inmates and ultimately set the tone and operational mode for each BOP facility. As a result, it is important to know whether the background factors used and the weights assigned to them are accurately assessing the nature of the inmates involved. For that reason, the BOP's Office of Research and Evaluation conducted a review of the elements used to determine custody classifications. The initial classification elements developed from staff surveys and mock classification exercises were found to be valid predictors, and ongoing research has assisted in fine-tuning point assignments and other predictive aspects of the system.

Beyond empirical validation, it is also important to track the results of actual implementation. Research and practical findings confirm the system's beneficial effect in virtually every dimension. Discretionary transfers between institutions that sometimes had adverse consequences in terms of inmate conduct or population balance have ceased. Inmate transfers as a whole were reduced dramatically, reducing those costs. The system is confining inmates in appropriate security level facilities, thus improving the efficiency of resource allocation in the BOP with respect to site acquisition, facility construction, staffing, and program planning.

The Classification System's Effect on Violence

How has this system affected violence in federal prisons? Anecdotal accounts abound of the stabilizing effect of the more homogeneous institutional climates in BOP institutions. Empirically, however, it is not possible to prove very much, if anything, about events that do not occur. Implementation of this system was accompanied by upgraded staff training, the spread of unit management, and other factors that confound the picture. However, the BOP's stable violence and escape rates during a time of extreme institutional crowding—up to 160 percent of capacity in the past few years—suggest that the classification system is at least partially responsible.

Although there were very few unanticipated consequences of implementing this system, one was the effects of the accumulation of the BOP's most dangerous, escape-prone inmates at the U.S. Penitentiary in Marion, Illinois, which previously served as a specialty penitentiary. By 1980, Marion's population began to show adverse signs of this concentration, and in late 1983, the institution shifted to a highly controlled program that involved high levels of staff supervision and a greatly reduced level of inmate movement. Although a broad range of programs and services is still available to inmates at Marion, the institution is the final resource for the BOP in managing this small but highly intractable group. Marion's deterrent effect is well-recognized by both inmates and staff, and low violence rates there and in other institutions support the proposition that it is serving its intended purpose.

The Evolution of the BOP's Classification System

Despite the system's initial and subsequent successes, a number of adjustments have been made over the years. A task force has met periodically to ensure that the structure of the system continues to meet the needs of BOP staff. These adjustments have included changes in the points assigned to various scoring elements, changes in the types of offenses included in some categories, and the addition of public safety factors. These were, for the most part, minor improvements to an otherwise sound system.

In 1987, new federal sentencing legislation took effect that dramatically changed the way inmates are sentenced, eliminated parole, and substantially reduced available good time credits. This, in turn, caused a major shift in the effect of sentences, which are now far longer in actual time served than those imposed under the former sentencing statutes. A ten-year sentence under the new sentencing procedures meant an inmate would serve about eight and one-half years with no possibility of parole, where formerly parole was a possibility after three years and four months and good time release was a virtual certainty at six years and eight months.

Moreover, increased law enforcement activity in the area of drug offenses meant that many incoming inmates had histories of sophisticated methods of introducing and distributing large quantities of drugs. These changes in inmate profiles made it critical that the BOP once again fine-tune its classification system.

Further adjustments to point allocations, scoring ranges, and public safety factors were needed to bring the system in line with the new sentences and types of inmates being encountered. The numerical security level structure was replaced by a minimum, low, medium, and high nomenclature for institutions. The concept of multicustody administrative institutions has been continued, and an "administrative maximum" security institution to replace Marion was commissioned.

A well-conceived classification system gives prison administrators a tool for developing other effective inmate management systems. In the

BOP, there are a number of related systems that help agency staff in their day-to-day management activities.

The BOP's automated information system, called SENTRY, is used as a vehicle for initial designation activity, which includes requests for designation, calculation of classification categories, and transmission of designation orders. SENTRY is also used to document the information gathered about individual inmates through the classification process in the institution and in subsequent reclassification actions.

The Central Inmate Monitoring System (CIMS) is a SENTRY-based system for tracking offenders whose cases present unusual management issues. Public concerns flowing from pretrial publicity, involvement in large-scale criminal enterprises, witness security cases, or unusual levels of criminal sophistication often cut across classification categories. However, CIMS permits staff to track such cases to ensure proper levels of management review are applied in every decision.

The BOP's classification system also helps staff manage crowding—a critical problem in most correctional systems today. Through the classification system, internal housing assignments can be made more effectively, and the array of BOP institutions can be strategically adjusted to meet the profile of the population. Proper monitoring of the system allows managers to ensure necessary balance is maintained between institution security levels and offender characteristics. As planning proceeds for expansion and renovation of existing institutions and construction of new facilities, projections of security and custody levels of the future population are critical. Having a clear picture of the nature and needs of the inmate population five or ten years from now is important when deciding how to apportion scarce resources.

Conclusion

The BOP has developed a rationally based classification system that serves as a cornerstone for its planning and inmate management programs. Although every system of this type needs continual refinement to meet the needs of its users and to adjust to changes in the inmate population that it serves, it is well worth the effort. Effective classification plays a central role in BOP correctional management.

X. The Future of Classification

By Lorraine T. Fowler, Ph.D.

Classification in regard to securing and supervising offenders is rooted in punishment. Many criminologists would agree with Hawkins and Alpert (1989) that American and British criminal justice systems originate from, and still resonate to, five punishment rationales:

> ...the retributionist rationale is based on the principle of deserved punishment as earned by the offender's past law violation. Just deserts are seen as a way of achieving equity, a balanced fairness between the offender and society, by imposing a cost (punishment) to offset the illicit gain (the crime)....
> The basic assumptions of utilitarian proposals [on the other hand, use punishment] to achieve one or more of these objectives:
>
> A. Incapacitation: Imprisonment isolates the offender, preventing the commission of crime by the offender in the community.
>
> B. Specific deterrence: Imprisonment will serve to make the inmates fearful of sanctions so that, upon release, they will refrain from further criminal activities because they wish to avoid reincarceration (fear of punishment).
>
> C. General deterrence: Imprisonment is used to set an example for the law-abiding, so they will continue to refrain from law violations.
>
> D. Rehabilitation: Imprisonment provides a setting where

Lorraine T. Fowler, Ph.D., is director of Resource and Information Management for the South Carolina Department of Corrections.

inmates will change their procriminal attitudes, their life-styles, and their propensity to commit crimes. The successfully rehabilitated prisoner will refrain from future criminal involvement for reasons other than fear of punishment.

Some of these objectives may conflict.... But the common link between all four is the future utility of punishment for reducing the crime rate.

Incarceration as punishment was prominent in the eighteenth and nineteenth centuries in Europe and America. Preferred punishments (other than death by hanging, burning, drowning, crucifying, stoning, and drawing and quartering) were often community-oriented and inclusionary (e.g., stocks, whipping, forced labor, torture, fines, and combinations thereof) or community-oriented and exclusionary (e.g., banishment, transportation, and sale into slavery). Imprisonment tended to be a temporary situation for an offender sentenced to one of these punishments.

The 1601 Elizabethan Poor Law established the notion of the "worthy" poor and the "unworthy" poor. The parish structure legitimated by that law distinguished between "indoor relief" and "outdoor relief"—between confinement in parish facilities and assistance provided in the recipients' own domiciles. Thus, indoor relief—originally almshouses for the legitimately needy and workhouses for the "shiftless, able-bodied" needy—took the form of workhouses or "houses of correction."

During the Industrial Revolution in the eighteenth and nineteenth centuries, parishes could no longer contain or sustain their poor—worthy or unworthy. Laws such as the New Poor Law of 1834 stipulated that the only relief to be granted to the able-bodied poor would be employment in workhouses. Thus, by the late nineteenth century workhouses were conceived essentially for punishment and forced labor (Frederico 1980), much like the "work gangs" of the twentieth century.

The Prison Congress of 1870 was revolutionary in the history of corrections in that it tried to radically alter classification and resultant circumstances:

The class consciousness indicated by the study of crime and punishment in [ante-bellum] South Carolina...is evidenced in the varying character of the punishments awarded "persons of quality," who were fined almost invariably, and "citizens of little respectability," who received public lashings and served jail terms.... It is displayed in the general evaluation of misdemeanors by the better classes as innocent amusement or understandable self-defense, whereas similar mis-steps on the part of lower-ranked citizens were designated as crimes against the State (S.C. ETV, et al. 1993).

If punishment as retribution is the sole purpose of incarceration, then bringing classification beyond social class discrimination is perhaps less relevant to corrections than sorting according to rational criteria is to, say, food or clothing warehouses. However, the separations of worthy from unworthy, the able-bodied from non-able-bodied, and then of male from female took on a very different aspect with the first Prison Congress. As Hawkins and Alpert (1989) imply, the principles of particular traditions of British and American religious and utilitarian reformers coalesced in 1870:

1."offenders" were to be differentiated from their fellows, but their "needs," their willingness to participate in their own "reformation," their ability to be integrated or reintegrated in the community were to be considered when punishment was determined;

2. offenders were to be separated in prison on at least the bases of age, sex, and seriousness of their crimes;

3. education, industrial training, assistance in return to the community were to "rehabilitate" in the spirit of John Howard, the English reformer of the 1770s: "It is doing little to restrain the bad by punishment unless you render them good by discipline."

These extraordinary innovations established the "ideal" agenda for U.S. (and Canadian) "houses of correction" until the "nothing works" movement gathered serious momentum in the 1970s.

Twentieth Century Classification

It is in the reformist tradition as delineated above that Kane in his chapter, "Classification: Its Central Role in Managing the Federal Bureau of Prisons," declares that classification is now, in the 1990s, commonly accepted by state and local jurisdictions as useful, even necessary, and it is in the same tradition that these entities make the following assumptions:

1. Sound criminal and personal information (beyond age and sex) are essential.

2. "Least restrictive" placement consistent with public, staff, and inmate safety lessens both risks to persons and confinement costs.

3. Inmates with similar historical and behavioral characteristics housed together are easier and cheaper to manage.

4. Public safety is always the primary criterion for "sorting" when that is our primary mission.

According to Kane, "The goal of classification in most correctional settings...is to ensure public safety, promote efficient management, and enable staff to manage their institutions in a cost-effective manner. In correctional systems experiencing growth, a further reason emerges for having a sound classification system—to assist planning staff in determining the type of expanded capacity that is needed, ensuring that the types of beds constructed meet the actual [rather than subjectively presumed] needs of the inmates."

That such objectives have been set and striven toward by more than one state jurisdiction is evident in Austin's "Objective Prison Classification Systems: A Review" and Baird's "Objective Classification in Tennessee: Management, Effectiveness, and Planning Issues."

Despite early twentieth century efforts of such pioneers as Burgess in Illinois, as Austin recounts, until very recently (the 1970s), modern offenders have been "sorted" or "classified" according to subjective opinions of correctional staff. Sometimes some of the staff were trained in social history and/or psychological assessment, sometimes not; sometimes security designations and custody placements were made by a team that essentially consensualized decisions. Since the development by the federal Bureau of Prisons of a system that classified both offenders and placement entities (institutions, community programs, etc.) and by the National Institute of Corrections of the NIC Model, about one-half of state jurisdictions (plus the District of Columbia) has adapted one of these models to create an objective system.

As Baird's discussion of development, progress, and problems in Tennessee shows, objective systems, reliably applied, offer clear, consistent criteria for allocating offenders to groups so that offenders in each class are similar, whether in regard to risk of unstable and/or dangerous behavior, to personal "need" characteristics, or to both. Thus, Belbot and del Carmen in their chapter, "Legal Issues in Classification," say that, presently, the weight of case law clearly shows:

> Courts recognize that although inmates do not have a constitutional right to a classification system, classification systems may be necessary to provide inmates with their institutional right to a reasonably safe and secure living environment (*Grubbs v. Bradley* 1982). Many prison and jail reform lawsuits have led to the implementation or revision of classification schemes to include criteria that clearly establish rational and reasonable grounds for classifying inmates and procedures that mandate the manner in which the criteria are to be implemented.... Classification is tantamount to the nerve center of inmate management.

Although correctional professionals coming to agreement on both clear, firm criteria and reliable, consistent use of them certainly may result in grouping offenders so that the variance within each group is less than the total variance and, thus, the process could be labeled "classification," as Sechrest has said, "The problem, of course, is that the definition is neutral with respect either to the basis of classification or to the variable or variables in which similarity is produced (or variance reduced)" (Gottfredson & Tonry 1987).

The variables chosen, the weight each is given, and their structure (e.g., additively, decision tree, etc.) cannot be neutral. Correctional classification, as Brennan in "Risk Assessment: An Evaluation of Statistical Classification Methods," states, must come to terms not only with objectivity, but also with validity, specifically around issues of risk assessment if the primary mission is to ensure the safety of public, staff, and offenders.

Ambivalence about Validation

Objectivity is not enough. All practitioners, researchers, and, certainly, researcher-practitioners have seen consensus that resulted in the emperor having no clothes when the consensualized opinion was that the emperor, indeed, had magnificent new clothes. Implementation of classification systems in jurisdictions using only this criterion has resulted in very costly redos and even more costly litigation. Fortunately, the Gottfredsons (1982), Kane (1986), Brennan (1987a, 1987b), and others have been willing to take on methodological and data quality issues because they understand that the "no clothes" issue is the critical issue, truly the *sine qua non* of effective classification:

> In operational terms, validity is a question of whether the classification system does what it was designed to do—consistently and equitably for all inmates. First, to perform risk assessment—that is, based upon specified assessment factors, each inmate's level of risk of involvement in serious disciplinary problems, especially violence and escape, is estimated. Second, to assign the inmate membership in a group characterized by a likelihood of involvement in misconduct commensurate with his or her own. Third, to minimize misconduct by managing each group with the security (structural) and custody (staff supervision) restriction deemed appropriate (Kane 1986).

Kane emphasizes that validation of instruments is different from validation of classification systems, the latter requiring recognition of, and attention to, systemic variables and environmental context. If there is one major future investment that must be made in correctional classification, it is that all jurisdictions should be supported in doing both process and impact studies of their systems. As Aiken points out in his chapter, political consensus is clearly an essential beginning, but implementation without validation has become infinitely more costly in many locales, discernibly in dollar terms, than it would have been had validation been done prior to, or with, wide-scale implementation (and were revalidation occurring on a periodic, systematic basis).

Brennan's chapter summarizes briefly the many studies that have supported, and that continue to support, the superiority of statistical assessment over practitioner/expert judgment, especially in the area of correctional risk. The fact that quality data, sensitive techniques, and capable consultants are now available renders inexcusable any jurisdiction's unwillingness to undergo rigorous evaluation, including validation, of its central administrative management tool—its classification system(s). As Brennan says:

> The bottom line…is that even in their present state of development, statistical risk assessments offer sufficient predictive validity in comparison with practitioner decision making, that there could be substantial upgrading of the decision processes in applied corrections if they were properly implemented.

Only Tough Issues to Tackle

Serious evaluation, including validation efforts, of classification systems with the purpose of determining cost effectiveness of both operational management and capital development should certainly be the primary future correctional initiative. However, other auxiliary initiatives, just beginning to be taken seriously primarily because costs are out of control, are critical.

Burke and Adams' (1991) recent work on the classification of female offenders points out that nothing much has changed since Brown, Nesbitt, and Argento's 1984 work: few systems classify women with any thought to the gender issues pertinent to objectivity or validity. Thus, the conclusion in Fowler's chapter, "What Classification for Women?":

> Evaluations of [the few] existing systems to which some thought and resources have been given, say in South Carolina, Illinois, or Wyoming, might well be a place for the National Institutes of Justice and of Corrections to begin to assess, design, research, and promulgate models for testing whether females and their communities can be served well at this stage of classification art and science.

Preliminary work in both the United States and Canada suggests a need to test the hypothesis that were "risk" rightly assessed and equitably applied to women, between 60 percent and 80 percent of female offenders could be most cost-effectively served via alternatives to incarceration. If this assumption were to prove true and subsequent appropriate action were taken, theoretically other public service systems costs for women and their children could be avoided or, perhaps, reallocated.

Women, if consciously managed at the front end of classification system(s) at all, are usually treated as a subset of the larger classification system. Whether that tactic is legitimate or not, a legitimate general subset of an overall system that assesses primarily for security/custody risk is internal classification for day-to-day management of not only all similar-risk, but all similar-needs offenders.

As Austin, Baird, and Neuenfeldt point out in their chapter, although Bureau of Prisons, National Institute of Corrections, and "offspring" models increasingly group inmates according to general risk level increasingly effectively, even with more and more minimum placements:

> within each classification level considerable variation still exists with respect to the inmates' criminal orientation, living

stability, likelihood of recommitting crimes, emotional needs, level of education, work skills, honesty, and other factors. To deal effectively with this variety of people and problems...both an understanding of the individual and flexibility in applying different supervision and programming techniques is [sic] required.... Staff who develop a better understanding of inmates and utilize greater flexibility in applying different supervisory and programming techniques may be more effective in managing inmates and controlling prison violence.

Their chapter, which recounts Washington's and other jurisdictions' experiences with the Prisoner Management Classification (PMC) and Client Management Classification (CMC) systems, suggests that large jurisdictions especially would benefit from developing, assessing, and implementing internal (institutional or unit or workload) as well as external (systemwide) systems. Particularly as staff and program resources become both more constrained and more stressed and strained, forming specialized units to supervise offenders with similar risk/need profiles makes more and more sense.

Summary

Future classification system efforts will pay off the resources invested in these critical management control tools if the following are done:

- current systems are subjected to competent process and impact evaluations (including strenuous validation in Brennan's sense)

- gender issues, explosive though they may be legally, managerially, and programmatically, are recognized and dealt with empirically and equitably

- serious efforts to maximize staff and general program resources are tested, using Adult Internal Management System, PMC, CMC, one of these in combination with unit management, or any similar method of ensuring that intrainstitution transactions are as cost-effective as are interinstitution transactions as a result of a thoroughly tested external classification system

- classification systems development and testing transcend not only gender issues but also such artificially imposed separations as in/out and institution/community; truly cost-effective corrections are not only systematic, but systemic—a continuum of control

What's Next?

Almost everything summarized to this point has been either initiated and implemented in the United States or initiated in the United States and occasionally adopted/adapted in various Canadian jurisdictions (e.g., PMC and CMC). In fact, however, Canada's federal jurisdiction has been supporting a clearly habilitative approach to corrections. Its investment, both fiscal and programmatic, has been long-term. The habilitative ideal so drives Canadian correctional approaches that many of the types of classification efforts discussed here are not simply irrelevant, they are openly rejected. Classification as we know it becomes subsumed by case management/case planning using an essentially cognitive model of intervention on an individual offender basis.

Canadian classification experts claim only that their model may help a substantial number of offenders; they deny the notion of panacea. What is critical for the future of classification, in North America at least, is that as we look to develop, test, implement, and evaluate our classification systems, we understand fully what it is we intend them to do: is "containment" of both people and costs really the only issue in this post-Nothing Works era? Is it possible that we in the United States need to reevaluate all that we have done in the most radical way?

References

Alexander, Jack, and James Austin. n.d. *Handbook for evaluating prison classification systems.* San Francisco: National Council on Crime and Delinquency.

American Correctional Association. 1982. *Classification as a management tool: Theories and models for decision-makers.* College Park, Md.: American Correctional Association.

Austin, James. 1986. Evaluating how well your classification system is operating: A practical approach. In *Crime & Delinquency* 32, No. 3, ed. Lawrence A. Bennett. Newbury Park, Calif.: Sage Publications.

Brennan, Timothy. 1987a. Classification: An overview of selected methodological issues. In *Prediction and classification: Criminal justice decision making*. Chicago: University of Chicago Press.

Brennan, Timothy. 1987b. Classification for control in jails and prisons. In *Prediction and classification: Criminal justice decision making*. Chicago: University of Chicago Press.

Brown, Aaron A., Charlotte A. Nesbitt, and Angela R. Argento. 1984. *Female classification: An examination of the issues*. Washington, D.C.: National Institute of Corrections.

Burke, Peggy, and Linda Adams. 1991. *Classification of women offenders in state correctional facilities: A handbook for practitioners*. Washington, D.C.: National Institute of Corrections.

Fowler, Lorraine T. 1993. *Classification of women offenders*. Columbia, S.C.: South Carolina Department of Corrections.

Frederico, Ronald C. 1980. *The social welfare institution: An introduction*. Lexington, Mass.: D. C. Heath and Company.

Gottfredson, Don M., and Michael Tonry. 1987. *Prediction and classification: Criminal justice decision making*. Chicago: University of Chicago Press.

Hawkins, Richard, and Geoffrey P. Alpert. 1989. *American prison systems: Punishment and justice*. New York: Prentice Hall.

Kane, Thomas R. 1986. The validity of prison classification: An introduction to practical considerations and research issues. In *Crime & delinquency* 32, No. 3, ed. Lawrence A. Bennett. Newbury Park, Calif.: Sage Publications.

Sechrest, Lee. 1987. Classification for treatment. In *Prediction and classification: Criminal justice decision making*. Chicago: University of Chicago Press.

South Carolina ETV, et al. 1993. *Our brother's keeper: CCI*. Columbia, S.C.: S.C. ETV, S.C. Humanities Council, S.C. Department of Corrections, S.C. Budget and Control Board, S.C. Office of the Executive Director, and S.C. Office of the Governor.